What others are saying about this book:

"More Americans put families ahead of work. Family is important to Patrick Snow. He is a speaker, coach and author of *Creating Your Own Destiny*. Employees used to be willing to sacrifice because of things like stock options. Now they're fed up. They realize that family is the only stabilizing force in today's turbulent economy. Making time for family isn't just important for a few employees like Snow—it's a growing priority for many workers disillusioned by layoffs, corporate scandal, and waning corporate loyalty. Seventy percent of employees don't think there is a healthy balance between work and personal life."

USA Today
Cover Story, December 5, 2002

"*Creating Your Own Destiny* is the ultimate resource for anyone who is unhappy at work and wants more out of life—full of real-life stories and strategies on how to get exactly what you want out of life!"

T.J. Hoisington
Professional Speaker and Author
If You THINK You CAN!
www.GreatnessWithin.com

"I am constantly looking for books that are well-written, resonate with our coaching approach of life-work balance, and that I can recommend to our clients. In writing *Creating Your Own Destiny*, Patrick Snow has produced a book that accomplishes all three. I like his balance between simplicity and insight. The book is a tremendous resource for anyone who wants to get started on living a life with purpose, direction, and fulfillment."

Raymond Gleason
Executive Coach, Building Champions, Inc.
www.BuildingChampions.com

"Patrick Snow has written the definitive guide to fulfilling your dreams and goals. Full of real-world insights—and solutions—to help you reach for and realize your destiny."

Cynthia Kersey
Professional Speaker and Author, *Unstoppable*
www.Unstoppable.net

"Patrick Snow's experience and insights run deep. His desire and passion drive him to help you make a difference in your own life."

Albert Mensah
Professional Speaker and Author,
When the Drumbeat Changes Dance a Different Dance
www.QuestForYourBest.com

"Patrick Snow knows what he is writing about when it comes to achieving ones' destiny. Highly successful himself, he has the real-life experiences to help take your life to the next level, and beyond. I strongly encourage you to invest in yourself—and in your destiny—by reading this book. It will change your life!"

Chris Widener
President, Made for Success, Extraordinary Leaders
Author, *Made for Success*
www.MadeForSuccess.com

"If you know what you want out of life, but aren't sure how to get it, this book is for you! Loaded with insights you can use right away."

Larry Olsen
Professional Speaker and Author,
Break Through to a Life That ROX!
www.myLIFErox.com

"*Creating Your Own Destiny* is a must-read if you are serious about living your dreams! Patrick Snow's strategies will make a tremendous difference in your life."

James Malinchak
Professional Speaker and Co-author,
Chicken Soup for the Athlete's Soul
www.Malinchak.com

"Want to realize your destiny? Start here."

Bob Rosner
Author, *Working Wounded* and *The Boss's Survival Guide*
Internationally Syndicated Columnist
www.WorkingWounded.com

"You know what you want—now here's how to get it! Read this book to get going on the life that you see in your mind everyday. *Creating Your Own Destiny* shows you how to get exactly what you want out of life!"

Dennis Mitchell
Professional Speaker and Co-Author,
Chicken Soup for the African American Soul
www.YesYouCanSucceed.com

"In writing *Creating Your Own Destiny,* Patrick Snow has discovered what I learned in my first Race Across AMerica victory. When you are doing something that you are truly passionate about, you produce a seemingly endless flow of energy from within your heart that gives you the ability to accomplish anything that you desire. Patrick's book not only shows you how to discover your passions in life, but also offers proven strategies to overcome your fears and eliminate all the roadblocks which stand in your way and hold you back!"

Danny Chew
Two-Time Race Across AMerica (RAAM) Champion
Million-Mile-Man Bicyclist
www.DannyChew.com

SUBARU JACK,

DREAM, PLAN, EXECUTE,

AND SOAR!

Patrick S____

A Success Road Map for High Achievers

CREATING YOUR OWN DESTINY

*How to Get Exactly What **You** Want Out of Life*

PATRICK SNOW

AVIVA
PUBLISHING

DEDICATION

I would like to dedicate this book to my family:

To my beautiful wife, Cheryl: Thank you for being so supportive of me in my many endeavors over the years! I appreciate you sticking with me through the good times and bad. <u>I Love You Dearly</u>!

To my children, Samuel and Jacob: You are the reason that I work so hard. This book is written for you. I hope that long after my time, you and your children will benefit from this message. <u>I Love You Both</u>!

To my parents, Jack and Lois Snow: You are the best parents a child could ask for. I have become the person I am today because of you both. Thank you for all the positive words of encouragement that you have so kindly spoken to me my entire life…I was always listening! I have benefited not only from all that you have given me, but also from all that you could not. <u>I Love You Both</u>!

ACKNOWLEDGMENTS

I would like to recognize and thank all of the following people for their support, encouragement, and belief in my dreams. I would also like to thank all of those listed here who have helped me with this book and my speaking career:

Robert Allen, Dave Beauchamp, Les Brown, Mike Bumpers, Alex Carroll, Kathi Dunn, Susan Friedmann, Raymond Gleason, Victoria Gonzales, Mark Victor Hansen, Michael Helgeson, T. J. Hoisington, Kim Hornyak, Jerry Jenkins, Charlie Jones, Paul Kadillak, Cynthia Kersey, Ellen Keszler, Harvey Klinger, James Malinchak, Bill McCarrick, Keith McKinnon, Ashoke and Kris Menon, Albert Mensah, Dave Nelson, Shawn O'Gara, Brian Olive, Larry Olsen, Professor Jack Padgett, Tim Polk, Dan Poynter, Sophie Ramsey, Anthony Robbins, Bob Rosner, Paul Schuler, Larry Sears Jr., Tom Snow, Ivey Stokes, David Torres, Paul Travis, Ted Treanor, Graham Van Dixhorn, Rob Van Pelt, Tobin Van Pelt, Tony Wall, Jim and Barb Weems, Mary West, Mike West, Chris Widener, and Zig Ziglar.

There are several others of you as well, you know who you are...

SPECIAL ACKNOWLEDGMENTS

I would like to give special thanks to Og Mandino, who through his book *The Spellbinder's Gift* inspired me to write *Creating Your Own Destiny*. *The Spellbinder's Gift* covers the life of a successful professional speaker, Patrick Donne. I won't ruin the story for you, but Patrick came to realize that people remember only 10 percent of what they hear. For this reason, he realized that by writing words down in print, more people, over a greater period of time, can learn and grow from his knowledge. *The Spellbinder's Gift* is the most inspiring book that I have ever read. My book began simply as nothing more than a road map or compass intended for my children. However, as I continued to write, it turned out to be much more… something that I felt destined to share not only with my children, but with others as well.

I would like to thank Mary West for all of your hard work in promoting this book and for setting up seminars and speaking engagements for me. You are awesome!

I would also like to give a special thank you to my editor and project coordinator, Tim Polk. Thank you, Tim, for all your help in organizing this manuscript. Without you, this project may never have been completed. You're the greatest!

Lastly, I would like to give a special thank you to Tony Wall (www.ToneDogStudios.com) for your expertise in creating my Web site, audio CD, and video. Contact Tony, if you are in need of web, audio, or video work done in your business, as he is the best in the industry.

TABLE OF CONTENTS

BREAKING FREE

**"Your heart is born free:
have the courage to follow it."**
— William Wallace

A re you *unhappy at work*? Do you want *more* out of life? Do you want to experience *true freedom*? Are you really *free*? Are you doing each and every day what your heart is calling you to do in both your professional and personal life?

I speak in front of thousands of people every year, and when I ask that question very few people raise their hands. Why? Most people aren't free. They've become a slave to their job or their life circumstances. They struggle with the things one "must" do: paying off credit card debts; working a full-time job (or even two jobs); taking evening classes; supporting a family and raising children; living from paycheck-to-paycheck.

Even successful people aren't immune from believing they're "trapped"—most people I know who make a lot of money become slaves to that financial success; the more they make, the more they spend, and thus the more additional money they need to make! I've come from a very modest middle class family, and I've also achieved financial successes far greater than most people. At times, I have also severely struggled financially and not known where my next paycheck was coming from. My faith in God has helped me overcome many adversities in my life. I have learned that money in and of itself doesn't make a man or woman free.

Over the course of a dozen years, I have interviewed thousands of disgruntled and unhappy employees across North America and learned that we all want the same thing: We all want *more* out of life! Most people basically want six things: more *time*, more *money*, more *freedom*, more *health*, more *love*, and more *happiness* in life. How then, can each of us get *more* out of life and recapture, as William Wallace said, our "heart ... born free"?

I believe we become free when we create and then follow our *destiny*.

What is destiny? Webster's Dictionary defines the word as meaning *fate*. Look up fate in the dictionary and you'll see that fate means *the supposed force that predetermines events*. I believe that this *supposed force* is our **MIND** (or brain). If we use our mind properly by taking action and executing our ideas and the opportunities presented to us in the way that we are capable of, then **WE** truly can become the *supposed force* that predetermines the events that occur in our lives. Thus destiny means to me the ultimate purpose (fate) each of us has here on Earth. Destiny is what each of us, as unique individuals, are put here on Earth to do, to become. Our destiny resides within us. It is our freedom, the great potential we have, the *supposed force* waiting only for our minds to unleash it.

By the end of this book, I believe that you can discover your destiny. You will also learn how you can apply my ultimate **Success Secret** for life. This secret will show you how to achieve what my subtitle promises:

*"How to Get Exactly What **You** Want Out of Life."*

I know what many of you may be saying: I can't influence my destiny. My job sucks! I'm worried about being laid off! My boss is an idiot! My credit cards bills and student loans are too high! Or, I have to work two jobs just to make my rent or pay my mortgage—and I can't even *think* about saving the down payment for a house like my parents owned while I was growing up. That's wrong thinking. Regardless of how bad your current circumstances are, you can influence your own destiny. You can shape it, make it become real. I'm going to show you how in this book, *Creating Your Own Destiny*. In this book, you will learn how to dream again. Once you are dreaming again, I will show you how to plan and execute to fulfill your dreams. As a result, you will soar for the rest of your life.

Still not certain? I don't blame you—believing we can influence our destiny requires huge thinking, an even bigger amount of belief. But each of us can think, right? Each of us can believe, right? Right—each of us can positively influence our fate. As Robert Ringer stated in his book, *Million Dollar Habits*:

> **"When your mind believes something to be true, it stimulates your senses to draw to you the things, people, and circumstances necessary to convert the mental image it houses into its physical reality."**

I believe this is how you create your own destiny. Your dreams can come true, in other words. As Abraham Lincoln once said:

> **"You become what you think about."**

There's something else that also often holds people back in the pursuit of their dreams: **FEAR**. Following your dreams can be scary. You might be rejected. It will take hard work. There will be obstacles along the way. But you must risk pursuing your dreams to become free. You will learn a strategy to put your fears aside once and for all!

I'm also going to encourage you to pursue the biggest dreams possible, the most (seemingly) impossible "things." Why? I strongly believe what George Elliot once said:

"Only those who will risk going too far, can possibly find out how far they can go!"

This book contains 12 chapters that will help you create and realize your destiny—and, I firmly believe, allow you to have more *time*, more *money*, more *freedom*, more *health*, more *love*, and more *happiness*. I call these 12 chapter headings my **Success Road Map**.

This concise road map has been written to show you how to be courageous in your endeavors and proceed in a manner in which you are truly capable. There is a saying by Ralph Waldo Emerson that goes:

"Do not follow where the path may lead; go instead where there is no path, and leave a trail."

You can blaze a new trail! This book will be your compass and help guide you along the way.

Before we begin, I think it's also important that you know that all the material here has been developed through my life experiences, which includes reading more than 1,000 self-help books, working in high-tech sales, being a motivational speaker and success coach, and most importantly, being a son, husband and father!

Please know that this book is more than just my thoughts and suggestions. What you are holding right now is one of my dreams come true! I believe that my destiny is, among other things, to help people overcome their personal fears and adversities to "set their hearts free."

I also believe that there is no such thing as a completed education. Education is a lifelong process. In fact, I believe that I can learn as much from you as you can from me. There is so much yet for me to learn — this is one of the reasons why I enjoy reading. I challenge you to become a lifelong learner and open your mind to the new ideas, strategies, and techniques offered in this book, and many others.

I want to challenge you to think like a world champion. If you knew that under no circumstance could you fail, what is it that you would attempt to do with the rest of your life?

I know what some of you may be thinking. *Patrick, achieving dreams is easy for you. You're successful, have all this great experience, plus you have a wonderfully successful and supportive wife and two great kids...but I, on the other hand, am too young (or too old) and too broke and inexperienced to accomplish great things.*

Whether you realize it or not, I am more like you than you might think. I have been a "struggling underdog" my entire life and only recently have experienced the realization of my vision. I am NOT there yet! I am a "work in progress." I continue to fight like hell in the arena of life to achieve my goals. On the other hand, if you have already arrived, then there is no reason for you to continue reading this book! If you are like me and continue to experience adversity in life, then let's move forward together in pursuit of our destinies.

I sincerely believe that if I can work toward achieving my destiny, that anyone can! Anyone—I repeat anyone can influence and enhance their destiny. What's more, let me say this: I believe you have what it takes to influence your destiny. How do I know this? I was once in your shoes, feeling apprehensive about following my dreams.

Also, based on the fact that you're taking the time to read this material and apply the following ideas and suggestions tells me you have what it takes to reach your destiny. And finally, every negative can also be a positive. You may believe you are too young, or too old, but think about it this way: You have the benefit of getting a fresh start with each new day. You have your whole life ahead of you to ACCOMPLISH GREAT THINGS! Now is the time to get started moving in the right direction.

Like I said and will say throughout this book, I want to help you. I will be your coach along the way, your guide, your confidant. If I can do it, so can you. I believe in you!

Think about what author, Nobel and Pulitzer Prize Winner Pearl S. Buck has said:

"The young do not know enough to be prudent, and therefore they attempt the impossible—and achieve it generation after generation."

I am going to offer you a quote, from Julius Caesar, before we begin:

**"For lack of training, they lacked knowledge.
For lack of knowledge, they lacked confidence.
For lack of confidence, they lacked victory!"**

In *Creating Your Own Destiny*, I am going to help give you the training, knowledge, and confidence to win in your own game of life!

Finally, as you read this book consider the following quote from Oliver Wendell Holmes, which reveals the tremendous power of our mind as we continuously grow:

"Man's mind once stretched by a new idea, never regains its original dimension."

This book will help you uncover new ideas, get out of your box, expand your comfort zone, and help you pursue the things in life you love. Additionally, you will learn to overcome rejection and put aside your fears as you pursue a new direction in life.

I wish you well on your new journey in pursuit of creating your own destiny…

Are you ready to begin? Good—let's go!

Patrick Snow
Bainbridge Island, WA
July 2004

CHAPTER 1

Visualizing Your Dreams

"Only those who can see the invisible, can accomplish the impossible! The BELIEF in your VISION is the key to Creating Your Own Destiny!"
— Patrick Snow

People who are successful in all areas of life—in their faith, family, business, sports—share a common trait: the ability to look into the future and visualize exactly what they want to accomplish. Here's what St. Augustine had to say about visualization:

"Faith is believing what you do not see. The reward of faith is to see what we believe."

Why is vision so important? Being able to visualize what it is that you want to do or accomplish paints a mental picture for your brain. Ever heard of the phrase, "Seeing is believing"? I'm sure you have. When we can "see" something, even in our minds, we're much more likely to make it happen. Another way to think of this is by what author Alex Morrison once said:

**"You must clearly see a thing in
your mind before you can do it."**

Let me tell you one way how visualization has changed my life.

I grew up the fourth of five kids in Owosso, Michigan, 90 miles northwest of Detroit. My father was a teacher, my mother a nurse. I was blessed with a loving childhood. I also was encouraged to pursue any worthy goal that I wanted.

Well, at an early age I decided that I wanted to play professional football! I can remember as a young child watching the Pittsburgh Steelers win multiple Super Bowls. I used to put my number-32 Franco Harris jersey on my black lab named "Bear" and then "practiced" my tackling techniques— although mostly what I did was to chase him around our backyard in the snow!

I was always small for my age but that didn't stop me. I quickly began to live by former Alabama football coach Bear Bryant's expression (which I still believe to this day):

**"It's not the size of the dog in the fight
but the size of the fight in the dog."**

I went out for the football team in the fourth grade and was very lucky to receive some great coaching all the way through high school. Even though most of the time our high school had very average teams, my senior year I led the team in tackles, interceptions, and fumble recoveries; was named Most Valuable Player; and also was selected as first-team all-league linebacker.

Looking back on this time, I must say that this was no honorable feat since my senior year we finished 0-9. To make matters worse, on Halloween night 1986 both our team and the opposing team had the same dismal record: winless at 0-8. Well, not only did we lose this game (which was termed the "toilet bowl" by our few loyal fans), but we lost in double overtime. Talk about a humbling experience! I learned that night that life is not fair and it never has been. I am sure that you can think of times in your life when you worked really hard for something and you still fell short of your goal. The point is that we need to learn from our disappointments and move on by developing a "NEXT" philosophy. In sales, I refer to it as "Some will, some won't, so what, NEXT."

My high school play earned me financial assistance to Albion College, a small Division III school in southern Michigan, between Detroit and Chicago. It wasn't the University of Michigan or Notre Dame, but I was still convinced that I could continue to develop my football abilities and eventually make it to the pros. I could see it in my mind, so I knew that it could happen!

But something happened during my freshman year at Albion, something that would drastically change the course of my life forever.

Before training camp, I was so eager to make a good impression on the coaches that I over-trained. Several of my rib heads would "slip out," i.e., become dislocated from my spine. A trainer would easily pop them back in, so I continued to practice with the team for almost ten days.

But things got worse as training camp progressed. We were practicing four times a day. At times I thought I couldn't breathe, the pain was so bad. Also, I couldn't raise my arms above my head. But I kept on, because football was my "life."

And then, just like that, my football career was over! I finally listened to the team doctors and chiropractors who said that no amount of rehabilitation could prevent the injury from reoccurring.

At first I was devastated! My dream since the fourth grade was now gone, dissolved in an injury that couldn't be stopped from happening again and again.

Fortunately, though, I was taking a Philosophy class at the time. One of the assigned books in particular had me fascinated: *Man's Search for Himself,* by Rollo May. The plot of this book, in a nutshell, is very similar to the William Wallace quote in this introduction: we are all born free; however, if we don't act upon this freedom by cutting the psychological umbilical cord to our parents early in life, we will only go so far. Or, to think of this another way, we'll be tied down like a dog on a chain in the front yard, only being able to go as far as the length of the chain allows us.

Once I understood this concept, I knew that my career-ending football injury wasn't an ending—it was a beginning! I was now free to go anywhere, to create a new vision for my life, to do new things. With the help of Rollo May, I had learned that there were bigger things in life for me than the game of football!

My back injury gave me a chance to start all over again, pursuing a new set of goals. Two of which were to become a motivational speaker and published author while pursuing a career in the field of personal growth and development to help others succeed.

Exercise

Can you think of a time in your life that seemed to be an "ending"? What were your thoughts, feelings, and emotions at that time?

_____

_____

_____

_____

Did this "ending" lead to a new "beginning"? What happened?

_____

_____

_____

_____

Of the current challenges you face today, are any of these disguised as an opportunity?

_____

_____

_____

_____

A NEW BEGINNING

I knew that I had only decided on Albion College because of my dream to one day play professional football. Now that my college football career had ended, staying at Albion didn't make sense. I hadn't yet had time to think much about my future and what I wanted to do, but I knew that I loved the mountains and that I wanted to explore the western part of the United States. So I sent an application to the University of Montana and was accepted.

Therefore, on January 1, 1988, as an 18-year-old college freshman who didn't know a soul west of the Mississippi River, I jumped on a Greyhound bus with a $69 ticket to transfer schools.

I didn't know exactly where I was going with my life, but I was confident that I was moving in the right direction.

And do you know what? Transferring to the University of Montana was the best thing that ever happened to me. I not only graduated with a degree in Political Science, but, more importantly, I also met a wonderful woman named Cheryl Monaghan—who later, I'm lucky to say, became my wife!

We now have two boys, Samuel and Jacob, and established careers: Cheryl as a Prosecuting Attorney for King County in Seattle, and myself with my speaking, coaching, writing pursuits, and a life dedicated to helping others succeed.

Let me say this: regardless of how exciting it would have been to play professional football and maybe even win a Super Bowl ring, it could NEVER equal the love I have for my family. My experience also has led me to be a firm believer that people must never set their sights on only one goal. It's too limiting. Instead, each of us should create a destiny that we're moving toward, a series of people and places as well as milestones that we want to accomplish in our lives.

Therefore, since I can't play in the NFL, I now have a new goal: to own my own NFL franchise by age 50. How is that for visualizing a dream? I will have to raise close to $500 million to achieve this vision, but I have almost 15 years to do so. I will be awarded an NFL expansion team. My team will be called the Hawaii Sharks and will play its home games at Aloha Stadium in Honolulu starting by the fall of 2018. If I can't get a fan base in Hawaii, then my other plan is to purchase the Seattle Seahawks. If you are interested in being a part of this NFL franchise and ownership group, I am currently accepting investment capital at the P.O. box listed on the inside cover of this book.

Depending on your thought process, you are either roaring with laughter, or buying into my vision! Either way, these are the kinds of visions that you must develop in your life. Your visions are invisible and possibly unrealistic to others, but they must become visible in your mind and heart so that you can transform the impossible into the probable!

After I attain the goal of becoming an NFL owner, on several occasions, I have dreamed of making a run at the office of President of the United States. What is important here is that if I desire to become President, then I believe it is a goal that I could attain. Ultimately however, I don't know if I want to expose my family to a life of constant public scrutiny. Additionally, I have a goal to sell one million copies of this book. I don't know exactly *how* I am going to accomplish any of these achievements, but I will cover the *how* later in this chapter.

After reading this last paragraph, you may be thinking that I have an ego the size of Texas. Well, I can assure that this is not the case. I believe there is a big difference between having a big ego and being self confident! My parents raised me to believe that I can accomplish anything in life, *if* I worked hard enough at it. Therefore, my persona of being an eternal optimist can be blamed on them. As a result of being raised this way, I believe that I do not have large ego, but I may have the highest level of self confidence of anyone that you may have ever known! There is a big difference between these two types of personalities.

If you further developed your level of self confidence and were to stretch your mind to believe in the power of your visions, what could you achieve in life?

It may not be a best-selling author, NFL owner, or even President of the United States, but your vision is uniquely important to you and that is why you are such a special person! Focus on your uniqueness of being your own individual, instead of allowing societal pressures to have you conform to becoming like everyone else. To set you free, you must develop faith in yourself and believe in your visions like never before.

The point about my new beginning is that *if I did not have the ability to dream big and envision what my future could be, then I never would have had the courage to board that bus to Montana.*

Because I was able to see the invisible, I have accomplished the impossible—a wonderful family, a successful career, and an exciting future!

I challenge you to develop your own visualization skills and see in your mind—your biggest dreams! Later in this chapter, I will show you *how* to turn your dreams into a reality—but before you can do this, you must understand that visualization is the first step.

When thinking of our futures, we need to learn to walk by faith, not by sight! Most people think that vision is something that you exclusively do with your eyeballs. I believe that vision is also something that you do with your heart.

EXERCISE

Therefore, if you knew that you could not fail, what would you envision your future to look like? Dream big and fill in your visions below:

_____

_____

_____

_____

_____

A PERSONAL MISSION STATEMENT

One way I've found to help visualize my ultimate destiny is to create a Personal Mission Statement. What is a Personal Mission Statement? In the 1990s it became fashionable for companies to apply for and receive ISO certification. This is a process that a company would go through to document everything that they do, with the idea being that organizations with sound processes and quality products and services could be identified. Part of the ISO process is for a company to create a mission statement: what is it that we as a company want to do and what is it that we as a company stand for?

I suggest you create something similar. In one paragraph, describe what it is that you want to "do" here on Earth during your lifetime. What do you want to focus your efforts on? Be remembered for? Work towards?

On the following page is my Personal Mission Statement written in July of 1997. I've since modified it slightly, but this will still give you a sense of what I believe your mission statement could look like. I have also included my mission statement for my business, The Snow Group, Inc., on page 32.

As you can see, a Personal Mission Statement is really about who you are and what you believe in. To help you get started thinking about your own Personal Mission Statement, think of these things:

- What do you want to be remembered for in life?

- What do you want your grandchildren to say, think, or believe about you?

- What do you believe in?

- Why do you work?

- What is your higher calling in life?

- What changes do you need to make?

- What are your visions?

- What are your dreams?

- What is your destiny?

MY PERSONAL MISSION STATEMENT

I dedicate myself from this day on to improve the world as much as possible by being:

- A strong individual who is a man of God

- A loving, faithful, and supportive husband to my wife

- A positive role model, strong influence, and best friend to my children by teaching them values, discipline, respect, self-esteem, confidence, and love, as well as giving them the freedom to explore the world

- A grown child who will make my parents proud, and someday reward them for their love and for helping teach me how to become successful

- A positive influence to those who aspire to grow on a personal and career basis through my motivational speaking, coaching, Web site, tapes, books, and other written materials

- A positive influence to young people who are beginning to make decisions about their own future

- A successful business owner

- A philanthropist helping those in need

- A happy, positive person with a good sense of humor

- A caring and forgiving human being

MY BUSINESS MISSION STATEMENT

THE SNOW GROUP, INC.

My vision as a business-ownership advocate is to help millions of people become successful in life by showing them how to overcome their fears, transform their passions into their own businesses, and ultimately create their own destinies! These "destiny students" will break free from their dependence on their job, and experience more *time, money, freedom, health, love,* and *happiness* in life as a result of becoming successful business owners. I will give back to those in need donating my time, money, and energy to help the youth of today become the leaders of tomorrow!

Patrick Snow

AUTHOR

SPEAKER

COACH

ENTREPRENEUR

(800) 951-7721

www.CreateYourOwnDestiny.com

EXERCISE

Create your own Personal Mission Statement. This may eventually take up one full sheet of paper.

MY PERSONAL MISSION STATEMENT

Name: _____ Date: _____

_____

_____

_____

_____

_____

_____

_____

_____

_____

DETERMINE YOUR DESTINATION IN ADVANCE

You must know what you want to accomplish before you can begin taking specific steps to make your dreams and destiny a reality. This reminds me of our last flight to Hawaii. My family and I boarded the airplane in Seattle bound for Honolulu. After the flight was airborne for some time, the pilot made an announcement: "Ladies and gentlemen, I have two pieces of news for you. One of them is good, and the other is not so good. The good news is that we have a 200-mile-per-hour tailwind, so we're making great time! The bad news is that we're HOPELESSLY LOST somewhere over the Pacific, and we have NO IDEA where we are!" The pilot went on to try to calm the passengers by adding, "We may not know where we're going, but we sure are getting there awfully fast!"

Now in this case, we did make it to Hawaii safely. But similar things happen to us all the time, don't they? Does your life feel at times like a lost plane, hurtling through the sky (life) "awfully fast" but also hopelessly lost? Many people are like this. Being able to visualize exactly what it is that you want to accomplish in life is a way to prevent this. Visualization gives your mind the ability to chart out your destination in advance (just as flight crews do every day).

Think about it: How is it that planes from all over the world are able to traverse across the largest ocean on earth only to land in Hawaii on a tiny speck of land? There are many correct answers, but the best answer for this example, is that the pilots of all of these planes have predetermined their destination in advance.

<u>I believe that we are also programmed with the ability to predetermine our destination in advance. We do this by creating a vision in our mind, then taking daily action toward our vision, and NEVER giving up, despite what everyone else says we can or cannot accomplish.</u>

I urge you to tap into your inner visions and predetermine your destination in advance. What is your vision for your life and where are you going? It is never too late to change or adjust your course—even if you are already in mid-flight. These mid-flight adjustments are part of the reality of flying. The same holds true in life. What mid-life adjustments are currently needed in your life?

Visualization (the ability to see the invisible) is what allows you to live out your dreams and become fulfilled in life. A lack of visualization steers you down a course which leads to nowhere. A place where you are not in control and a place where resentment is sure to set in, because you've ended up somewhere you never wanted to go!

This reminds me of one of my favorite quotes from an unknown source:

"The road to someday leads to a place called nowhere!"

I challenge you to take action now and live by the Personal Mission Statement you've created *on a daily basis*. Note the emphasis. Anyone can create a mission statement and then do nothing to make it a reality—a vision that never becomes real because no actions are taken. Successful people know that action—on a daily basis—must happen to make your vision become a reality.

The ability to visualize your dreams will give you the confidence to pursue and fulfill your biggest goals in life! In fact, Toni Ann Robino, a friend and mentor of mine, has said that:

"When your dreams DIRECT your life, your life REFLECTS your dreams!"

Simply ask yourself "what was it that you wanted to become as a child?" Once you recall this memory, then ask yourself if your heart still wants this out of life? If so, dream big and pursue this passion with all your heart! If not, soul-search for your new beginning, then pursue your current passion with all your energy and don't let anyone's ignorance or negative attitude stop you short of seeing your light at the end of the tunnel!

SUMMARY

To conclude this chapter, I will now share with you *how* to accomplish your visions. I want to share with you the knowledge of a man who has really helped me take visualization to a higher level. I met Larry Olsen, author of *Break Through to a LIFE That ROX*, about three months after the first edition of this book was published. Larry's expertise on **VISION** has helped me answer the question *how* one accomplishes their visions. I am eternally grateful for his mentoring of me. Larry's book is a *must read*, as it teaches you how to create a vision for yourself three years out, and then live that vision NOW! My favorite quote from Larry Olsen is as follows:

"I have no right to work on the 'HOW' until I can taste, touch, smell, feel, hear, emotionalize, and 'OWN THE VISION.' The vision comes first and then I see 'HOW' to accomplish my dreams!"

According to Larry, as soon as you own your vision, the *how* (in terms of how to turn your goals and dreams into a reality) will *always* appear!

For example, I had no idea *how* I was going to write this book, but the *how* presented itself slowly over time once I learned to own my vision and developed an unstoppable mentality toward what I wanted to achieve. Similarly, today I have no idea how in the world I will become a NFL team owner, a bestselling author, or maybe even President of the United States one day. But as I learn to own these visions, the *how* will again present itself—just as it did with writing this book.

Most importantly, none of my visions will just happen for me, unless I first set them as goals. As a result of turning my dreams into goals, there is always a chance that my visions will come true. Without doing so, there is NO chance at all! The same principle holds true with your dreams. Someone will attain your visions, why not you! Always remember this anonymous saying:

"If not you, then who?"

What are your visions? I encourage you to think about your visions day and night. If you can do this, you will eventually take ownership of your visions and the *how* will magically appear! If you follow this strategy, then you are destined to get exactly what you want out of life!

CHAPTER 2

Setting Big Goals

"There is a time when we must firmly choose the course we will follow, or the endless drift of events will make the decision for us."

— Herbert Prochnow

In the first chapter we discussed vision and how to achieve your dreams. We talked in big-picture terms, sweeping—even grand—landscapes, very broad in nature.

Now it's time to get more specific. We do this by *setting* and *prioritizing* our goals.

Definition: A goal is the progressive realization of a dream in a given time frame.

In other words, goals are specific elements, if you will, of our big-picture vision to accomplish or complete within a set time period. If our destiny is a skyscraper, goals are the bricks and steel beams that serve as the building's foundation.

Because this is the case, it's imperative to understand that goals are the foundation to realizing the destiny for which you were born. Your goals are the key factor in determining the events that occur in your life.

The following is a Successories quote on goals, which I believe drives this point home best:

"Effort and Courage are not enough without Purpose and Direction."

Goals (which come from purpose and direction) are something that we can only create from our heart. Many times, people get overwhelmed by the vastness of their biggest goals, and question themselves by asking questions like, "Is my goal realistic, or am I just dreaming?" "Should I listen to all those people who are telling me to just give up and settle for mediocrity?"

I believe that you should not just set your sights on your ultimate goal. It is far easier to just concentrate on your next challenge, and then proceed toward your ultimate destination one step at a time. Otherwise, it is too easy to become overwhelmed by the overall goal and give up. Many years ago I wrote down this quote from an unknown source that ties into this point very well:

"Goals are not promises, but commitments. They are not wishes, but visions.

And we do not dream and hope these dreams Are going to find us; we find them.

Your goals don't start in your brain; They start in your heart."

The beautiful thing about goals is that you have a choice: to build and create your own destiny, or to sit back, like

Herbert Prochnow says, and let life's circumstances determine who it is that you become and what you achieve in life. I believe that those who decide to "sit back" are like a leaf blown off a tree during a windstorm that flutters aimlessly until landing at an unknown destination. These folks end up falling to wherever it is that the wind blows them...beaten up and battered, eventually stomped on and crushed! I know this may sound harsh, but think about all the people in this world who have never done something significant, and who then end up regretting later in life all that they WOULD'VE, COULD'VE and SHOULD'VE accomplished. Remember: "almost" only counts in horseshoes and hand grenades!

A SPECIAL NOTE

I was very lucky in my life in the fact that my father, Jack Snow, a high school science teacher and golf coach, introduced me to the concept of goals and having a written goal sheet when I was in the eighth grade. His comments must've hit home with me, because I've updated my goals every year since then! I'm eternally thankful for his guidance and support.

THE POWER OF GOALS

The goals of a person define who that person will become and what that person stands for! Only those who set goals in sync with the visualization of their destiny will achieve their destiny. Simply put:

<u>Your goals define YOU!</u>

In order to establish your goals, of course, you must be clear on what it is that you want in life. W.L. Hunt once said that:

"The first key to success is to decide exactly what it is you want in life."

Goals should have these traits:

- They should be written down. Write down your goals, then keep them handy to review frequently.

- They should be specific. A goal such as this is too vague: "I want to make more money." Instead, make your goals as specific as possible: "This year I want to generate $50,000 in my home-based business."

- They should have a built-in time frame, for measurement purposes. Again, avoid this: "I want to save enough for a down-payment on a house." Instead, write your goal like this: "I want to save $x by December 31, 200x for a down-payment on a house."

- They should be reviewed and updated on a regular basis. Reviewing your goals frequently keeps them fresh in your mind. Plus, as events in your life change or as you reach certain goals, you'll want to update your master goal sheet. I keep my goals inside my daily planner; other ideas include attaching them to a calendar, keeping them in an "important information" file, or in another location where you'll be sure to see them frequently.

Earl Nightingale was one of the early forefathers of goal research. Here is what he said on the importance of goal setting:

"People with goals succeed because they know where they're going."

At some point in your life (I'm hoping that point in your life is RIGHT NOW) you must search your soul for the answers to the questions that follow. I call these my **Life-Defining Questions.**

Please note that you should take your time thinking about and then answering these questions. Don't rush through this. The quality of your thinking and answers will go a long way in the ultimate quality of your goals.

If you don't have enough room or you don't want to write your answers in this book, I encourage you to order my *Destiny Journal Workbook*, which is a comprehensive 30-day program to self-discovery. The order form is in the back of this book. The workbook gives you plenty of room to write in all of your answers. You can also visit my Web site **www.CreateYourOwnDestiny.com**, then click on "Free Stuff" to print off all of the goal sheets to use time and time again.

LIFE-DEFINING QUESTIONS
Question 1: What are 10 things that I want "TO BE"?

1.
2.
3.
4.
5.
6.
7.
8.
9.
10.

Question 2: What are 10 things that I want "TO DO"?

1.

2.

3.

4.

5.

6.

7.

8.

9.

10.

Question 3: What are 10 things that I want "TO HAVE"?

1.

2.

3.

4.

5.

6.

7.

8.

9.

10.

Question 4: Where are five places in the world that I want "TO GO"?

1.

2.

3.

4.

5.

Question 5: What are 12 five-year goals that will help me accomplish questions 1-4?

1.

2.

3.

4.

5.

6.

7.

8.

9.

10.

11.

12.

Question 6: What are my 12 one-year goals that I must do to "get me on my way"?

1.

2.

3.

4.

5.

6.

7.

8.

9.

10.

11.

12.

Question 7: Where do I want to live?

(Be specific: what state, area, region? What type of house? What do you want nearby—water? the ocean? mountains?)

1.

2.

3.

Question 8: Who is the *one* person I want to make my journey with?

_____

This will most likely be your spouse. As you read this, however, you may not know who this person is yet...but if you desire to get married someday, simply write the word "spouse." Also, do you want to have children someday, and if so, how many? _____

The next thing to do in support of your one-year goals is to complete the "Monthly Goals" worksheet (see next page). This sheet is designed to give you the ability to achieve your one-year goals. In order to do so, all you need to do is to complete four or five smaller goals / tasks / projects each month that will lay the foundation for the success of your larger goals. Simply ask yourself this question: "Am I capable of doing just one thing per week?"

This monthly goal sheet can also be found on my Web site under "Free Stuff."

On page 49, you will also notice my "**50 Lifetime Accomplishments**" goal sheet. This goal sheet is designed to force you to look at your entire future, and then pick 40 to 50 things that you want to achieve. I encourage you to first list the 10 best accomplishments in your life to date. Then write what you still need to accomplish in numbers 11 to 50. You will be amazed by how focused you will become on your destiny as a result of completing this exercise.

MONTHLY GOALS

January

February

March

April

May

June

July

August

September

October

November

December

50 LIFETIME ACCOMPLISHMENTS

1. _____   26. _____
2. _____   27. _____
3. _____   28. _____
4. _____   29. _____
5. _____   30. _____
6. _____   31. _____
7. _____   32. _____
8. _____   33. _____
9. _____   34. _____
10. _____   35. _____
11. _____   36. _____
12. _____   37. _____
13. _____   38. _____
14. _____   39. _____
15. _____   40. _____
16. _____   41. _____
17. _____   42. _____
18. _____   43. _____
19. _____   44. _____
20. _____   45. _____
21. _____   46. _____
22. _____   47. _____
23. _____   48. _____
24. _____   49. _____
25. _____   50. _____

WHERE TO LIVE

Some of you may be wondering about Question 7, deciding where it is that you want to live. Let me explain why I believe this is so important to achieving your destiny.

Several years ago Marsha Sintar wrote a book titled *Do What You Love, The Money Will Follow*. I agree with her, but I also believe people should take her philosophy a step further: live where you want and the money will follow. Once you have visualized your destiny, then finding a place to live that is compatible with both your goals and your destiny is imperative.

For example, I had my first interview out of college at a company located in Seattle, Washington, in December 1991. I can remember looking west across Puget Sound and envisioning how wonderful it would be to live on Bainbridge Island. I loved Seattle, and I loved living near the water, so to me Bainbridge Island represented the "perfect" place.

But it also supported my goals. The island is very close to downtown Seattle, with its abundance of shops and restaurants—plus access to the University of Washington and Seattle's professional sports teams. Yet the fact that the island is away from the hustle and bustle of the city provides me the time to think and contemplate, write books (such as the one you're holding), and otherwise escape and recharge my batteries. It is also a terrific place to raise a family, since it has one of the best school districts in the state and there is virtually no crime.

Like most goals, though, living on Bainbridge Island took time and planning. When my wife Cheryl and I first moved to Seattle in 1991, we couldn't afford to buy a home on Bainbridge Island (or anywhere else, for that matter), so we found a place to rent about 20 miles northeast of downtown. But I continued to dream about living on Bainbridge Island. To help me visualize my dreams, we often went there on picnics, driving around, visiting the beaches, and otherwise soaking up the atmosphere. We also saved our money. Five years went by. My wife graduated from law school and became a prosecuting attorney in Seattle. My sales career had stabilized and I was fortunate enough to be able to work from my home office.

Therefore, in 1997, we bought a piece of land on Bainbridge Island to build our home. However, qualifying for the home loan was not as easy as we had hoped. We were approved for a certain amount prior to having the home built. During the construction process, we ended up adding on about $20,000 worth of upgrades. As a result, Carolyn Frame (the loan officer) was not thrilled because now the loan numbers did not balance out. Therefore, we now needed to show the bank some "contributing factors" in order to get the approval for the home loan. With this being the case, I opened up my calendar book and showed Carolyn all of my goals (which were in the same format that is outlined in this chapter). As a result, she said "now that I have seen your written goals—I can easily get your loan approved!" One of the goals that I showed Carolyn was to become a published author. As a result of having my goals written down, we were able to get our home loan approved because she could see that we did not pose a risk.

If you too had your goals written down, what is it that you would ultimately get in your life?

We now live very happily on Bainbridge Island. Another of my dreams has come true! But, as you can see, this dream supports my destiny of speaking and inspiring others; a person's goals and dreams must all interact—they must never be in conflict with each other.

My next goal is to buy waterfront property on Bainbridge Island and build my dream home, fully equipped with a custom-designed lighthouse to reflect my love of the sea and passion for lighthouses. I already have my land picked out, and soon I will take action toward the fulfillment of this goal!

Once this goal is attained, my plans are to purchase a waterfront condo on Kaanapali Beach in Maui, so that our family can spend the winters together in paradise.

What does your dream home look like? Where will it be located? What part of the country? I challenge you to envision each and every little detail of this goal, then take action so that you can achieve your dream!

A GOAL COLLAGE

Here's an idea to help make your goals seem more real, and thus obtainable. Create what I call a "goal collage." This is nothing more than a set of pictures that represent your various goals. Create this collage, then hang it in a prominent place, somewhere where you can see it often. Your office is an ideal spot for this.

A goal collage does two things: it provides a visual reminder of your goals, and once a goal has been realized, it gives you a sense of satisfaction and a stronger belief that you can meet your other goals.

Please note that I'm *not* talking about something small: my goal collage is two feet high by three feet wide! Go wild, get crazy—create something fun and big and exciting that will help you get excited about your dreams (cork bulletin boards work great). Try a goal collage—you'll be pleased with the results! Make sure that your goal collage includes a complete set of pictures of your dream home in the location that you desire to live.

SUMMARY

As I hope you see by now, having written goals is not a hindrance, a limiting factor, something that you "have to do." No, goals provide freedom in that your destination has been set and you are now free to actively pursue exactly what it is that you want in life. Just remember to have fun at all times. As the saying goes, "half the fun is getting there!"

I promise that if you complete your own life-defining questions, then you will not only lead a more fulfilled life, but you will also be in control of your destiny. Your goals will give your life purpose and direction! Therefore, your character will never be questioned because everyone (especially you) will know where you are, and more importantly, where you are going! Your goal collage then becomes a picture of what your future will look like, in the destination that you desire.

Finally, make certain NOT to create regret for yourself later in life. Don't die with *your* music still kept inside you! Set and prioritize your goals in a manner in which the world will hear you sing and feel your music, and ultimately, benefit from your efforts in one way or another!

CHAPTER 3

Creating Your Game Plan

**"The indispensable first step to getting
the things you want out of life is this:
decide what you want."**

— Ben Stein

B y now I hope you're feeling better about your destiny,
the positive things you can do and become in your life.
You've created a mental picture of your destiny and also written
down specific, attainable goals that support your vision.

But this next step is what, more often than not, stops
people from being successful. Usually one of two things
happen at this point:

- With so much opportunity and excitement possible,
  a person can't decide what to do first. They literally
  become "paralyzed with potential."

  or

- A person rushes full speed into one particular
  element of destiny, spending a whirlwind of time,

energy and money in a "let's do this as fast as possible" state. Like a runaway horse, though, this short burst of energy usually looks much more impressive than the results produced.

Jean Cocteau drives this point home with this saying:

"The speed of a runaway horse counts for nothing!"

What then is the answer? I believe it's simple: to create a game plan, or blueprint, to follow to help you navigate along the path of success. If you were starting out driving on a cross-country trip, would you begin without a map? Of course not. Nor should you begin moving toward your goals and destiny without a similar course of action in mind.

Another way to think of this concept is this: Many people who struggle with a sense of direction would not attempt a cross-country trip without some type of map and compass, to help them reach their ultimate destination. As we discuss destiny (a derivative of *destination*) and goals, it is important to utilize any tool or tools that can help get you where you want to go.

A compass (defined as a device for finding direction) can symbolize your goals. For example, if you determine that you want to travel north, then you will need a compass (goals) to tell you in which direction to travel. Without a compass (goals), you may want to travel north, but it will be extremely difficult to do so. Just as a compass was important for sailors crossing the ocean many years ago (and it's still invaluable today), so too are goals and a game plan for your long journey to your destination.

Former U.S. President John F. Kennedy provides the best example of someone setting a goal, taking ownership of a vision, and creating a game plan to accomplish this vision. In a speech before a joint session of congress on May 25, 1961, President Kennedy announced the ambitious goal for the United States to send the first man to the moon, and then safely return him home again. All of this was to be accomplished before the end of the 1960s. How is that for a vision?

This decision involved much consideration and an enormous amount of expenditures and human effort to make project Apollo come to realization in 1969. Shortly after this goal was announced, a tremendously ambitious game plan was created and then executed over the course of eight years with the efforts of the federal government, NASA, and engineers and contractors from all over the United States.

Tragically, President Kennedy did not live to see the realization of his goal. He was assassinated in Dallas, Texas, on Friday November 22, 1963. On July 20, 1969, Apollo 11 commander Neil Armstrong and Buzz Aldrin stepped off the lunar module and on to the moon's surface while millions of people around the world tuned in on their radios and televisions to hear the following statement: *"That's one small step for man, one giant leap for mankind!"* Shortly thereafter, the Apollo 11 team safely returned home again, and President Kennedy's vision was realized.

The game plan that was put into place on May 25, 1961 has forever changed the boundaries of what is possible in space exploration. If you were also to create a game plan in pursuit of your passion, and take action on a daily basis, what could you ultimately achieve in life?

This is a tough question, because if you are like most people, you may be thinking, "OK, I have dreams that I want to accomplish, but I have no idea how to even get started."

If this is the case, it is extremely important to work smarter and not harder by maximizing the power of your calendar book or personal organizer, and incorporate the use of flexible planning to improve the daily habits in your life. Finally, if you do all of the above and fully utilize the goal sheets that we discussed in the last chapter, you will become unstoppable and achieve what your game plan has put in place. Let's have a look at each of these components to creating a game plan.

WORKING SMARTER, NOT HARDER

Crawford Greenwald has said:

"Every minute you spend planning will save you three minutes in execution."

I'm a firm believer in the old saying that "Proper Planning Prevents Poor Performance." Have you ever wondered why the majority of people are either dead or broke by the age of 65? I think that one of the major reasons that so many people end up like this is simply due to poor organization, lack of planning, bad habits, and less-than-desirable time management. Most folks who fail in life don't plan on failing, they simply fail to plan! Studies have shown that many people spend more time planning their vacations than they do planning for their retirement!

I think no game plan is complete without the following three ways to work smarter rather than harder:

- Incorporating a high-quality calendar book
- Using "flexible planning"
- Developing habits that take control of your life

THE CALENDAR BOOK

A calendar book is one of your best investments to helping you execute your short-term game plan and long-term destiny. You must, as the old saying goes, "Plan your work and work your plan," and a good calendar book will help you do just that. Specifically, a calendar book allows you to list the tasks you need to do to accomplish your goals, and also break these tasks down into daily duties and responsibilities. Only when you live day by day and accomplish small tasks will you create something monumental over the long term.

Here are some key elements to the best calendar books and how to use them to their maximum potential:

- It should be a comfortable size *for you*. This is something you will want to carry with you virtually everywhere you go. Because of this, you'll want something small enough and flexible enough. Avoid trendy products or those that are too big or bulky to be carried. Some, for example, can be more than two inches thick. I believe these are not convenient enough to be carried at all times.

- It should be large enough. You are going to want to include a great deal of information in your calendar book. Not only your daily appointments, of course, but also your long-term goals, your Personal Mission Statement, and other destiny-related elements. Because of this, make certain that you purchase a calendar book that's large enough. I also like a large-sized format because I can comfortably glance at my calendar book when I'm driving. Again, find the size that works for you. I recommend a book approximately eight-by-ten-inches and less than one inch thick. I would also recommend the weekly calendar book from "Letts of London." Most fine office-supply stores carry these.

- Plan ahead. When you find a calendar book that's right for you, begin to look in October or November for the following year's edition. I find that I do a lot of planning for the coming year in December—you'll want the next year's book for this planning.

- Make certain that you only have one calendar, then record everything in it. I know this sounds pretty basic, but you'd be amazed at the people I've seen who keep a variety of personal organizers, wall calendars, and desktop calendars. I also strongly suggest you not solely use a computer calendar. Why? You want something that's convenient, that you can take with you. Even laptops require charging and are not possible to use in some instances.

- Don't separate work and personal information. This ties in closely with the first point. Again, people who want to achieve large, far-reaching destinies have goals that support both their personal and professional lives. Thus one calendar should be used to keep these two inter-connected areas tied closely together.

- Record your successes. Another positive attribute about a calendar is that it can become a record of your accomplishments, even a diary-like way for you to savor small triumphs. Recording and then later reviewing your "successes" is a sure way to increase your confidence. I have saved all of my calendar books and I can look back and tell you exactly what I did on any given day since 1991 when I graduated from college.

SPECIAL NOTE: SMART PHONES

Today's powerful new electronic tools are called smart phones. I think these tools are incredible resources to help you better communicate while on the road and become even more organized.

These smart phones are a cell phone, a PDA (personal digital assistant), a digital camera, wireless email, and Web access all in one unit that fits in the palm of your hand. They can also be used as platforms for reading e-books, which are becoming one of the fastest-growing segments in the publishing industry. E-books give you the ability to read day or night, without having to rely on lighting. You can read with one hand, and you can carry dozens of titles while traveling.

Calendar books still serve a place in your toolbox, because you can place photos of your family in your book, plus insert all of the goal sheets that you created in the last chapter. This way, you will have these reminders with you wherever go. Always keep your smart phone and calendar book with you!

FLEXIBLE PLANNING

A second element to mastering time is to implement *flexible planning*. I first learned about flexible planning more than 15 years ago from Charlie Jones. His book, *Life is Tremendous*, first introduced the concept of flexible planning to me. Without this knowledge, I know I would not be where I am today!

To do flexible planning, I suggest the following:

- Throughout the month consistently write down your deadlines, tasks, and responsibilities.

- Once you have all your "to do's" written down in your calendar book (not on loose paper or lists), simply prioritize each item in terms of its importance related to your daily successes. For example, you may have 10 main items written down for a particular day. All may look very time consuming, even perhaps overwhelming! But by prioritizing the items from most (1) to least (10) important, you can focus your efforts on a particular task. Please note that you may not complete all ten items (or whatever number you have) that day. That's fine—the next day, simply reprioritize your "to do" list based on what is yet to be completed.

As a result of following this strategy, each and every day you will always make progress by getting the most important things done first. Here is a short example of what my daily planner looked like on this day:

MONDAY, JANUARY 19, 1998

1⊠ 6:00 a.m. Aboard 5:30 am Ferry
(Bainbridge Island to Seattle-35 min.)

2⊠ 7:00 a.m. Alaska Air #2700
(Lv. Seattle @7:50 am, arrive Boise 10:05 am)

3⊠ 8:00 a.m. Read morning paper

4⊠ 9:00 a.m. Check voice mail

5⊠ 10:00 a.m. Call Dan (NW Customer Service Rep)

6⊠ 11:00 a.m. MCMS appointment

7○ 12:00 p.m. MCMS lunch

8○ 1:00 p.m. Mail monthly bills

9○ 2:00 p.m. Return phone calls

10○ 2:30 p.m. Hewlett Packard appointment

and so on...

You can develop your own system for checking off activities as they are completed. I recommend that you put a circle next to each activity, and then, rather than crossing out the entire activity once completed, simply put an "X" through the circle. This helps you when you need to refer back to previous dates—your activities won't all be crossed out and difficult to read.

A SPECIAL NOTE

You'll be, almost daily, removing and adding items to your main "to do" list. If you practice the concept of flexible planning on a daily basis, I guarantee you that you'll never miss another deadline. How many people can say that!

DAILY HABITS OF A WORLD CHAMPION

Habits are those things we do over and over. I'm a firm believer in programming myself to do certain things at set periods of time. If I plan correctly—again, there's that word "plan"—I'll be able to far surpass what I would otherwise be able to accomplish.

It's important to develop good habits in all areas of your life if you want to experience a tremendous amount of success.

The neat thing about habits is that studies have shown that if you work on doing something for 21 straight days, then it becomes a habit and you no longer need to work to do it!

As an example, on the following page is my "Daily Habits of a World Champion" sheet. You'll notice that I created four main categories: family, faith, wealth, and health in an attempt to lead a balanced life. Feel free to use these or make up your own.

***Execution* of your plan will be the difference between winning and losing!**

Today's Actions = Tomorrow's Results! This requires world-champion-performers to provide leadership in all areas of their life, by **balancing** family, faith, wealth, and health for the long term, while at the same time keeping the degree of a positive mental attitude that they desire their children to have when they grow up!

FAMILY	FAITH	WEALTH	HEALTH
Spend 2x time,$\frac{1}{2}$ $	Church on Sundays	Working 7am-6pm	Premium fuel only
Sat. nights w/ Cheryl	Daily reflection	Quick follow-up	No food after 7pm
Read boys 15 min.	Teach children	Want vs. Need	No snacks w/ high fat
Many family vacations	Church activities	No wasting time	8 waters each day
15 minutes kitchen	Accept what can't change	Diversification	Sleep 10:30 - 6:30
15 minutes laundry	Daily conversations	Project board	Walk 2 miles/day
Listen to needs	Co-pilot theory	Ownership w/o debt	Work out T,Th, Sa
Protect family	Give of time	Save accd. to plan	Stretch twice daily

GOAL SHEET INSERTS

Remember all those goal sheets that you completed in Chapter Two? Well here's another tip to successfully combining your goal sheets with your calendar: simply affix your goal sheets to the inside cover of your calendar book (and first few pages if necessary). You can also combine these goals onto one goal sheet as provided on my Web site: **www.CreateYourOwnDestiny.com**.

Now you can look at your goals on a regular basis—I strongly suggest *at least* several times a month! This continual reinforcement of your goals will sharpen your vision and help you as you prioritize your tasks and deadlines.

Another way to utilize your goal sheets is to check off or highlight with a yellow marker the goals that you have accomplished. Again, this positive reinforcement will show you that you can accomplish worthy goals and will give you the momentum and confidence to achieve other goals. Momentum is important because as it builds, it can become almost impossible to stop—think of small waves that, over a period of time, become a tidal wave!

To further enhance your calendar book, here are some other things that you may want to add to the beginning pages in addition to your goal sheets:

- Your Business Mission Statement
- Your Personal Mission Statement
- Pictures of your family and loved ones
- Your favorite motivational quotes
- Monthly goals
- Your goal collage
- Pictures of your dream home

Please note that it's extremely important to read your goal sheets often. Carrying them with you in your calendar book is an ideal way to help keep these handy. How many times have you found yourself with "free time" while on a plane, waiting in line, at the doctor's office, stuck in traffic, on hold on the phone, etc.? With your goal sheets handy, even "down" time can be turned into productive time.

Use your time wisely because you have a definite destination—the realization of your destiny! Just remember what Yogi Berra said:

"If you don't know where you're going, you are bound to end up somewhere else."

SUMMARY

Creating a game plan is essential for you to ultimately achieve your goals and your destiny. Let me leave you with a story about how I used a game plan for success.

My wife and I ultimately bought some land on Bainbridge Island, then we built our house. While it was quite an undertaking, we were able to create what we wanted from scratch. We now live in a beautiful custom-built 3,600-square-foot home. In addition to a host of wonderful features inside the house, we also have a half-court basketball hoop in our garage that includes:

- a 10-foot retractable rim with a fiberglass backboard

- a 16-foot-high ceiling and insulated walls

- 12 recessed canned spotlights

- two heating vents

- a regulation size key and free-throw line and key painted on the floor

As you can imagine, it's a great place for my kids and I to play basketball whenever we want. It's so large, in fact, we can also play catch with a baseball. Growing up, I never had a basketball hoop in our driveway, so I was determined to provide one for my children.

Did all this happen "by chance"? No, we had to plan and make decisions and prioritize at every step of the way. Our house and indoor basketball court are the result of many years of well-thought-out planning and execution.

In a sense I've created a small indoor gymnasium for my children. We play in there virtually every night all winter long and share a tremendous amount of fun and laughter.

The result of creating and following a game plan is simple: for the first time in your life, you will have a positive impact on the direction you want your life to go.

If you remain persistent in this process over a period of several years, you will realize that YOU—and not uncontrollable circumstances—hold the key to creating your own destiny! It's a wonderful feeling of freedom. I sincerely hope you experience it.

Once you have grasped this concept and incorporated this mentality into your daily life, then nothing in the world can stop you short of what it is in your life that you want!

Always remember that every winning game plan in life requires you to work smarter and not harder while incorporating three separate (but equally important) elements:

1. Calendar Book / PDA (<u>planning</u>)

2. Flexible Planning (<u>flexibility</u>)

3. Habits (<u>execution</u>)

CHAPTER 4

Building Real Wealth

"When prosperity comes, do not spend all of it."

— Confucious

In the last chapter we discussed the importance of creating a game plan. Many people have put together solid plans, but lack the financial wherewithal to accomplish their goals. They feel as though they need a tremendous amount of money before they can actually begin living their dreams.

Studies show that most people simply want more *money*, more *time*, more *freedom*, more *health*, more *love*, and more *happiness*.

However, most young folks today simply want a decent job so that they can save for the American dream of owning a home and having a car in the driveway. At the same time, most older folks simply want to achieve financial security, and someday be able to retire.

In this chapter, I will introduce principles and tools to show you how to get more money in your life *regardless of your age or current situation in life*. Additionally, if you play your cards right, more *money* will ultimately get you more *time* and more *freedom*. However, money cannot buy you more *health*, more *love*, or more *happiness*!

Money is important in this world. But too many people rely on gambling or lotto tickets because they believe this is the only way to get rich. This simply isn't true. Regardless of your financial circumstances, virtually anything that you set out to accomplish is still within reach. It may take you working one or two jobs for a time, or having a part time business. It may take a lot of work, in other words, but money is a necessary tool to create freedom. And freedom gives you the time to pursue your goals.

The key is to work smarter and negotiate more often. In this world, you either need to spend less than you make, or make more than you spend. Either way, you will spend much of your life negotiating something or another, so always remember to ask for more than you want to ensure that you will get what you need. Too many people get hung up working at their job, living paycheck-to-paycheck, and they never make the time to learn the principles of wealth creation and financial planning!

Our challenge then is simple: to get the retirement thing over with (invest enough money to retire) as early as possible, so that you can become free to pursue your destiny.

YOUR JOB IS A TEMPORARY VEHICLE

It's crucial to understand that a job is nothing more than a vehicle in which you position yourself to do two main things:

- Provide right now for your family
- Learn so that you can advance to the next level (whatever that might be).

Here's something I'm certain you don't often hear:

I believe that work is OVERRATED! That's right—I see work / a job as simply a method to support my family while I pursue my life goals.

Having this philosophy about work will help you in many ways. The old philosophy of going to work for a good company to get "job security" no longer exists!

Take a minute to digest the following alarming statistics about the status of job security workers level of discontent in today's day and age:

ABC News reported in September of 2003 that nine million Americans are unemployed.

USA Today recently reported that 50 percent of American workers say they are "unhappy at work," and the numbers are as high as 66 percent in New England. My friends in Canada tell me that the percentage of people unhappy at work is even higher there.

USA Today also recently reported that 70 percent of workers don't think that there is a healthy balance between work and personal life.

Gallup Organization shows 55 percent of employees are actively disengaged in their jobs—putting in their time but with little or no energy or passion. They neither identify with their work nor promote company objectives. This results in loss of productivity in the U.S. economy at more than $350 billion per year.

CREATING YOUR OWN DESTINY

CNN reported that in the year following 9/11 over one million Americans were laid off.

Center for Creative Leadership reports that 40 percent of new hires end in termination.

This is not a problem just in the United States. These same issues are a reality throughout most of the world. In fact, most of the working conditions worldwide are far more concerning than those in the United States. The above numbers prove that job security and workers level of satisfaction is a thing of the past!

Instead, if we are to make it financially today, we need to create "income security." What is income security? Income security can only be reached if you understand two main strategies about money and wealth, both of which I learned from multimillionaire Ivey Stokes, a successful entrepreneur who today is CEO and Chairman of a very successful Internet and e-commerce company. These two key strategies are as follows:

1. How to Get Wealthy in Today's Business Environment
2. How to Utilize Four Wealth-Creation Principles

MULTIPLE STREAMS OF INCOME

During my early days just out of college while working in corporate America, I soon realized that no matter how hard I worked on a job, my annual raises were minor— most in the five percent range. I soon also realized that if I were to accomplish the many goals that I have set out to achieve in life, I'd need to improve the vehicle (my job) that

I was driving. I would have to diversify, in other words, by creating multiple streams of income.

Multiple streams of income is really a simple concept: you have income coming in from more than one source. Ideally, the more income sources you have, the more total money you'll receive. In the stock market and in the world of investing, it is considered common knowledge to have a diversified and well-balanced portfolio. Since this is the case, don't you think it would make sense to also have a diversified income stream? Just as it doesn't make sense to have all your money in one stock, it also doesn't make sense to have all your income come from one source!

Here are ways my family creates multiple streams of income:

<u>Sources of Income</u>:   Motivational speaking fees

Success coaching fees

Coaching fees for publishing and book production

Sales of this book and audio CD

Sales of second book, workbook, and video

Day job income

Spouse's salary

Interest earned from investments

Residual income from a home-based business

BUSINESS OWNERSHIP

Another common source of additional income is starting a home-based business. Many people also have tried (and become quite successful, too) doing network marketing. Network marketing (also referred to as direct sales or multi-level marketing) is a legitimate way to diversify your income and make money working from home without having to invest a lot to get started. According to the Direct Selling Association (DSA), 11 million American's are currently involved in network marketing. Worldwide, many more millions of people have chosen this vehicle to earn money building their business from home. I have known several people in network marketing who have worked very hard and become multimillionaires from this industry, as well as others who have not worked at all and made almost nothing. As with anything else, you get out of network marketing what you put into it.

Twice I ventured into the world of network marketing. Over the course of about three years, I made a total of $12,000 working one night per week. Today I am no longer actively involved in network marketing (over the last five years, I have chosen instead to focus my efforts on my speaking career and book promotions), but I remain firmly committed to the idea of building other income opportunities in addition to my day job. However, many of my best clients are actively involved in this industry.

If you want to work from home and own your own business, but you are completely confused as to what kind of business to start, then I recommend that you visit my Web site **www.CreateYourOwnDestiny.com**. Click on "Free Stuff" to download and print a copy of :

50 Home-Based Business Ideas
(that you can start for less than $500)

When getting into business for yourself, you must be absolutely certain that there is a need in the marketplace for your company's product or service! This is one of the biggest keys to being successful in business, and a fair amount of research is needed to ensure success. There are not many folks selling 8-track tapes or typewriters any longer—you get the point!

Whether it be a result of owning your own business or doing network marketing, the goal remains the same—to build your business once, then get paid for life!

<u>IMAGINE what it would FEEL like to wake up in the morning and know that whether you rolled out of bed, or rolled over, all of your bills that month would be paid!</u>

What a great feeling this would be—business ownership is the only way to experience this feeling of more *freedom*.

A SPECIAL NOTE

All my extra activities are meant to produce income, of course, but they are also related to my life destiny and goals, which are to positively influence people through my motivational speaking, writing, and coaching. Always attempt, as much as possible, to combine generating additional income with your life goals and ultimate destiny.

IMAGINE FURTHER WHAT THE RIGHT BUSINESS CAN DO FOR YOU!

Imagine if you could take up to six months off each year and travel anywhere your heart desired without having to ask permission from your employer to do so!

Imagine if you owned the home of your dreams in a place that you always desired to live!

Imagine if you had a vacation home in addition to your dream home, which you and your family could enjoy for many generations to come!

Imagine if you had enough money that you could build your business out of choice instead of having to work at your job out of need!

Imagine if your children could go to college wherever they desired, instead of settling for a school you can afford!

Imagine if you could write a check each year for $100,000 or more and give it to your favorite charity!

Imagine if you could dedicate the rest of your life to helping others in need!

Imagine if you could experience the FEELING of having more *time*, more *money*, more *freedom*, more *health*, more *love*, and more *happiness* in your life.

Well, now you can turn *if* into *when*, once you start your own business in a field that you are passionate about, and sell your products and services to the public in large volume. It is just that simple. This is the formula.

The execution of this game plan on a daily basis is all that you need to do to achieve financial prosperity through business ownership.

I know what some of you may be thinking — that you know of business owners who have gotten started in business and are now stuck working 70 to 80 hours per week. They have no extra time and certainly no freedom. I agree that there are many business owners who find themselves trapped in this predicament.

However, the kinds of businesses that I endorse are businesses that you can own and operate from the comforts of home. For this reason, I have been called an advocate of home-based-business ownership for years. I also believe that you will be better off to contract out some of your needs as opposed to hiring direct employees.

I know what else you might be thinking — I have already tried business ownership in the past, but failed! The bottom line is this: All of us at one time or another have been left stranded at the side of the road with a car or truck that has broken down.

The reality is that we do not give up on automobiles and spend the rest of our lives walking everywhere just because we were once left stranded. Instead we just get a new vehicle. The same principle holds true with business ownership.

EXERCISE

Sit for several minutes thinking about ways you may be able to generate additional income in your life. Then list as many of these ideas as possible:

1.

2.

3.

4.

5.

6.

7.

8.

9.

10.

Now pick one. What next steps can you take to begin to put this idea into action? What can you begin doing *now* to make this a reality?

_____

_____

_____

_____

_____

A SPECIAL NOTE

Regardless of what you choose to pursue on the side, make certain that you do so without jeopardizing your day job's income stream. I have seen too many people get fired for doing their new business venture while on the clock at their day job. You must keep these completely separate! It has been said that you work nine to five to make a living, but that you work five to midnight to make a life! Lastly, make certain that whatever income opportunities you select, they are consistent with the following Wealth-Creation Principles.

WEALTH 101

According to a publication titled *Personal Wealth* from the Internal Revenue Service (IRS), in the early 1990s there was roughly $15 trillion in accumulated wealth in the United States. In a more recent study published by Merrill Lynch in late 2003, personal wealth within the United States had climbed to $27 trillion dollars. However, 90 percent of the wealth is owned by only 10 percent of the people! The question then must be:

What knowledge do the wealthy 10 percent have, that the other 90 percent are missing?

The answer is this: the wealthy 10 percent understand that the quickest way to wealth is through business ownership. They also know how to build themselves income-producing assets (by building ownership and equity). Let's explore each of these important concepts:

THE COMMON-SENSE DEFINITION OF WEALTH

According to Ivey Stokes, wealth can be defined as:

Owning "income-producing assets" that allow you to live in the manner that you desire, without having to work next week, next month, next year, or many years to come.

Wealth produced from these assets can support your family for many generations. Wealth, in other words, is a measure of the freedom it provides you—not your level of income. This is so foreign to so many Americans, who try to display wealth or give the perception of accumulated wealth through their high standards of living. Unfortunately, this leads to debt and a high-consumption lifestyle that inhibits ones ability to create an income-producing asset.

WHAT IS AN INCOME-PRODUCING ASSET?

To put it simply, something that pays dividends. An income-producing asset is usually a financial investment that pays you dividends (such as stocks and mutual funds). Real estate or a business that you own are also considered income-producing assets. Having a rental property, for example, provides you with a monthly source of income. In many cases, a combination of all the above become a solid income-producing asset. The concept here is to build an asset that will, for many years to come, generate income for you and your family. For example, if you build a $500,000 asset over several years which pays 10 percent annually, you would then receive $50,000 per year in dividends. If your lifestyle could be maintained on this amount, then you would be considered wealthy—even though you may not have millions of dollars in the bank—because you would then have the choice whether or not to ever have to work again.

WEALTH CHARACTERISTICS

Again, according to Ivey, most wealthy Americans <u>own</u> a business that sells products or services to the American people in <u>volume</u>. They understand that distribution is the key because volume requires reaching many people in many places.

Therefore, they partner with others to create wealth through mass distribution. This is vitally important to anyone who wants to be wealthy:

<u>The key to wealth is through ownership, not through a salary</u>!

One time, my oldest son asked me how to make lots of money. I thought it was a pretty good question coming from a fourth grader—I could tell he was not content with his current allowance! I replied by saying, *"All you have to do is to own your own business and sell products and services to the world's consumers in volume!"* He understood this right away—it's that simple!

Ivey uses Bill Gates as an example. Mr. Gates did not become the wealthiest man in the world because he was the best software writer; rather, it was because he was the best in the world at selling software in volume!

OWNERSHIP AND EQUITY

Significant wealth is achieved by earning or purchasing stock ownership in one or more companies during the early stages of your life, and then letting the stock or other ownership "investments" appreciate. In real estate, it's common knowledge to consider home ownership more beneficial than renting. If you agree with this statement, then why do so many Americans rent their skills on a job to an employer that doesn't provide stock options? A job then is really only renting, unless you build equity via stock options!

Therefore, if you are working at a job (while building your dream on the side), make certain that you find an employer that allows you to earn stock options. With stock options, you now become a business owner. As a result, you will do a better job and ultimately earn more money in the long run.

HOW DO I BUILD AN INCOME-PRODUCING ASSET?

Ivey Stokes states that the key is to execute his four Wealth-Creation Principles:

Principle No. 1: Business Ownership

Ninety-seven percent of financially independent Americans own businesses, which gives them huge tax advantages.

Principle No. 2: Asset Leveraging

Multiply your income potential through other people's efforts, time, talent, education, and leadership through selective partnerships. This allows you to, in effect, earn one percent of 100 people's efforts rather than 100 percent of your efforts.

Principle No. 3: Royalty / Residual Income

Expend effort once, and then receive residual income for years. A book or software program is a good example: a best-selling book can sell for years and years, yet the author only wrote the book once.

Principle No. 4: Taking Advantage of Trends

Positioning yourself in the right situation at the right time can make the difference. How can you take advantage of the up-and-coming trends?

Everything that I have learned in my life about wealth came directly from Ivey Stoke's wealth-creation philosophy. Because of this knowledge over the years, my family and I will benefit for a lifetime!

I also have learned over the years of another principle that I believe should be added to Ivey's four:

Principle No. 5: Knowing and Trusting the People with Whom You Do Business

There are many people who are like sharks, and are only in any venture for their own personal gain. Be careful with whom you do business. Over the years, I have discovered one way more than any other to determine who are the people that you can trust—and who are the people that you can't trust. It is simply by how a person looks at you. If while engaged in conversation a person continually looks away from you, they are either unsure of themselves or lying! Either way, you should avoid doing business with these types, unless you want to get burned down the road!

A SPECIAL NOTE

Two of the biggest drains on your finances are <u>taxes</u> and <u>interest</u>. It's mind boggling to track how much these two financial enemies steal from your household budget. I challenge you to sit down sometime and add up all the money that you spend over the course of a year on taxes (a good CPA can help minimize your tax burden), and interest (from credit cards, student loans, your mortgage, car loans, etc.). Once you have added this up, I encourage you to do two things to help minimize these "enemies":

1. Start a home-based business, which will reduce your tax burden

2. Borrow as little money as possible

ANOTHER DEFINITION OF WEALTH

Wealth can also be defined as having an abundance of financial and emotional peace of mind. This can be attained by having more *time, money, freedom, health, love,* and *happiness* in your life.

<u>**Your best shot of achieving wealth is to combine working from home with business ownership in *your* area of interest**</u>.

KNOWING WHERE YOU'RE AT

As you probably already realize, keeping track of your financial life can be complicated and challenging. Here's one item that I've developed over the years to help me keep a handle on my finances, and it just may help you as well. This also has become a tremendous tool for me to ensure that all my bills get paid on time each month. (See the Wealth-Creation Blueprint on the next page.)

According to the book *The Millionaire Next Door* written by Thomas Stanley and William Danko, your expected net worth should be as follows: 1/10 age x annual household income. I believe the Wealth-Creation Blueprint is a great way for you to see in one place all your investments, your liabilities, and your overall net worth. I update my blueprint every month. I also suggest that you list account numbers and phone numbers of the financial institutions for easy reference. I even use it to help pay bills—as a bill comes in, I log it; once it's paid, I cross it off.

Consider creating your own Wealth-Creation Blueprint to help you keep track of your financial future. Once you have created it, it's very easy to update monthly. It's gratifying to watch your assets grow and your liabilities decrease!

Remember, building real wealth does not happen overnight. It can take several years to get to a point where you never need to worry about money again.

Another great book on wealth is *The Automatic Millionaire* by David Bach who is also a *New York Times* best selling author of *Smart Couples Finish Rich* and *Smart Women Finish Rich*.

WEALTH-CREATION BLUEPRINT

PAYMENT	ACCOUNT #	PHONE #	BALANCE

ASSETS (Investments)

_____ House	_____	_____	_____
_____ Investments	_____	_____	_____
_____ Stock A	_____	_____	_____
_____ Stock B	_____	_____	_____
_____ And so on...	_____	_____	_____
_____ IRA	_____	_____	_____
_____ 401(k)	_____	_____	_____
_____ etc.	_____	_____	_____

Total: _____

EXPENSES (Utilities)

_____ Bill A	_____	_____	_____
_____ Bill B	_____	_____	_____
_____ Bill C	_____	_____	_____
_____ And so on...	_____	_____	_____

Total: _____

LIABILITIES (Loans)

_____ Loan A	_____	_____	_____
_____ Loan B	_____	_____	_____
_____ Loan C	_____	_____	_____
_____ Loan D	_____	_____	_____
_____ And so on...	_____	_____	_____

Total: _____

Net Worth =
Total Investments – Total Loan Balances: _____

SALES SUCCESS FORMULA

According to a sales trainer friend of mine, Brian Olson (www.RivendellGroupltd.com), there are only two very basic psychological reasons for people to make buying decisions. The two reasons why people buy are the *fear of loss* or *hope of gain*. My sales success formula will help you achieve more sales now that you know why buying decisions are made.

Whether your background is in sales or not, as a new business owner you must sell! Even if you have never sold before, you have sales experience, whether you realize it or not. How can I say this? Simple: Everyday we all sell!

We sell our spouse, significant other, parents, children, employer, and employees, on what a valuable person we are in their lives. This is selling, and it occurs on a daily basis!

How then can we all become better at selling in our own business given today's ultra-competitive environment? After more than a dozen years in business-to-business corporate sales, I have slowly learned and further developed a formula for successful selling. This Sales Success Formula has become my mantra.

When building a team, making a sale, or developing relationships, remember that trust (T), respect (R), and need (N) are all required to achieve success ($). Simply put:

$$T + R + N = \$$$

How then can we use this formula in all areas of our lives to achieve even higher levels of success (including making more sales for our businesses)? The answer is that people always love talking about themselves. Therefore, the best salespeople in the world have figured this out and try not to ever dominate conversations. The goal is to ask lots of questions, uncover customers' needs, and briefly explain how your business's products and services will solve their needs. Then it is absolutely necessary for you to shut up and let your prospects talk themselves into buying from you—while you are listening!

Listening is one of the most powerful tools in the field of business, but unfortunately it is rarely used to its fullest potential. You can't learn when you are talking! The bottom line is this:

<u>Friends buy from friends—people buy from those they like!</u>

If you want more sales, make more friends. It is that simple! The best way to do this is to talk less, and listen more. Ask thoughtful questions to get to know your prospects more deeply. As you do this, your prospects will grant you a deeper level of trust and respect. Then, if you can fill a need for them, you will earn their business in almost every occasion.

We need to speak 10 percent of the time, and let our prospects talk about themselves 90 percent of the time. If you put my Sales Success Formula to use in both your personal life as well as your business life, you will be amazed at how quickly you will attain a new level of wealth in both your relationships and your finances. As a result, you will get more *money* and more *love* in your life!

Doing What You Love

Building wealth is the key to obtaining the three things most people want: more *time*, more *money*, and more *freedom*—the freedom you need to eventually realize your destiny. I will discuss how to get more *health*, more *love*, and more *happiness* later in this book. In order for me to reach my destiny of helping others, for example, I will no doubt become more diversified and increase my wealth at the same time.

Many people overlook the importance of diversification in their lives. Remember that from an investment standpoint, at no time should you put all of your savings into one stock or one specific investment. With this in mind, why would you only have *one* source of income—your job?

When I ask this question, some have replied to me, "what would my employer think if they knew I had additional sources of income coming in?" My answer is simply this, don't tell them what you are doing in your home-based business!

Secondly, make certain that your own business does not interfere with your day job! Keep in mind that many presidents and CEOs are compensated one way or another by being on the board of directors of companies other than their own. My argument is simply that they do this primarily (among other reasons) for income diversity—so should you!

<u>Remember that your employer does not own you, they simply employ you because of your skills</u>.

You must diversify, whether it means taking a second job, starting your own company, or opening a home-based business. Only then can you begin the path to true financial freedom and wealth, and move rapidly toward your destiny.

However, to put wealth in a different perspective, I do want to warn you to stay away from the trap of materialism (trying to keep up with the neighbors). This can be catastrophic over time. After all, it was Socrates who once said:

"He is richest who is content with the least."

I challenge you to focus your energies each month on always improving your "Wealth-Creation Blueprint." If you do this, your debts will slowly decrease while your assets gradually increase. Over the years through the proper execution of the wealth principles discussed in this chapter, your financial challenges will be minimized.

The key is to soul-search for your inner passions, then turn these passions into an opportunity or a business that you can own. When you are doing what you love, you will NEVER again have to work another day for the rest of your life!

This will free you up to more thoroughly pursue your destiny and experience more *time*, more *money*, and more *freedom* as a result!

Doing what you love (in the context of building wealth) reminds me of what two-time Race Across AMerica (RAAM) winner, and million mile man bicyclist Danny Chew said after winning this event:

"When you are doing something that you love, there is a seemingly endless flow of energy coming from within your heart that gives you the ability to accomplish anything that you desire!"

For Danny, this belief allowed him to win the RAAM on two separate occasions—riding 21 hours per day for eight straight days. If you too, started doing what you loved, what would your *seemingly endless flow of energy* allow you to accomplish?

SUMMARY

Breaking your dependence from your day job and building real wealth is not easy, as you will learn from my experiences. However, as you tap into your new found energy, you are bound to start making more money as a result. Therefore, always remember the following lesson which my father taught me well: Just because you can afford to buy something, it doesn't mean that you always should! The goal is to invest as much money as you can in an emergency fund or investment portfolio, so that you can attain a greater level of peace of mind.

The more toys that you buy, the less money you have invested and working for you. This, in turn, means that you are earning less interest than you could if you learned how to spend less and save more.

Your personal finances and money are always at the center of building your wealth. If you like, you can view this as a game, a game that comes with serious consequences. Take *Monopoly*, for example. When you run out of money, the game is OVER. The same principle holds true in real life.

Therefore, our challenge is to never run out of money! This can be hard to do if you are like me: investing a tremendous amount of time, money, and energy into building a business to create an income-producing asset.

As a result of having invested so much of my income and savings into my business and getting laid off on two separate occasions, I had come very close to running out of money and finding myself in a "game over" situation.

We had our power, water, cable, home phone, business phone, and cell phones all turned off at one point or another. We almost had both of our automobiles repossessed. We also had been within a month or two of loosing our family home that we built back in 1996.

I am so thankful for my beautiful and supportive wife, Cheryl. Her salary as a prosecuting attorney kept our mortgage paid and put food on our table during these turbulent financial times. She was the saving grace that kept our family together given our challenging circumstances. I don't know if I could have made it through this adversity without her by my side through this process! She is truly an amazing woman, a talented prosecutor, and a loving mother!

These times were *excruciatingly painful* for my family and me! While my wife, kids, parents, and friends all kept their belief in me, many others who are very close to me gave up and even encouraged me to quit following my own dreams of becoming a best-selling author and world renowned professional speaker, and just get a job.

However, the BELIEF in my VISION kept me fighting, and now I have built my business into an income-producing asset that pays me thousands of dollars per day for speaking, coaching, and doing seminars! As a result of building this asset, I will NEVER again find myself in the financially dire straits I have been in at times over the last several years.

Most importantly, through this process I have become free since our family is no longer completely dependent on corporate America to support our needs.

Through this painful process of following my dreams, providing for my family, and trying to survive financially, I learned that nothing worthwhile in life comes without risk! I have also learned that if you remain committed to your visions, take daily action in pursuit of your goals, then NOTHING can stop you from achieving your destiny!

My challenge now for you is to do the same—follow your passions and build yourself an income-producing asset that will pay you and your family for life! The time is NOW and the BEST investment you can ever make is in yourself and your future! If you do this, you will build real wealth for your family!

EXERCISE

What can you do right now to invest in yourself and start building real wealth for you and your family?

_____

_____

_____

_____

_____

CHAPTER 5

Putting Your Family Ahead of Work

"Knowing who you work for, is priceless!"

— MasterCard® commercial

Have you seen the MasterCard® commercial where the father and son are at some exotic tropical island, swimming in crystal-clear water? As you watch this scene the narrator says: "Knowing who you work for, is priceless!" This is without question my favorite commercial. Why? That father has his priorities straight.

In the last chapter we talked a great deal about finances and building real wealth. But there is more to life than the pursuit of wealth. Money is important, but we'd also all agree that our children—and the children of the world—are far more important!

Ultimately when everything is said and done, very few people find themselves on their death bed wishing that they would have spent more time away from their family at work. In fact, just the opposite is true. Most people wish that they would have spent less time at work and more time with their family. From this day forward I challenge you to put your family ahead of work!

In doing so, you will learn the truth in one of my favorite quotations my mother recently gave me. This poem is for all you parents out there who struggle financially for your family but still manage to meet your children's basic needs of food, shelter, and love:

A hundred years from now...

It will not matter
What my bank account was,
The sort of house that I lived in,
Or the kind of car I drove—

But the world may be better
Because I was important
In the life of a child!

The problem is that so many people today are working so hard at their job that they can't spend quality time with their children.

This fact, combined with other difficult realities of working in today's economy, has led to an alarming increase in workers' discontent and level of unhappiness. Are you one of the 50 percent of Americans that *USA Today* reports are "unhappy at work"?

While making sales calls over the last dozen years, I have tracked corporate layoffs and interviewed literally thousands of disgruntled employees. As a result, I have compiled a list of:

THE TOP-10 REASONS WHY YOUR JOB SUCKS!

10. Not enough vacation time

9. No tax deductions as an employee

8. Unpaid overtime, and working on weekends

7. Business travel away from your family

6. Your daily commute

5. No respect and no job security

4. Too little pay and no ownership

3. Worrying about being laid off

2. You work with a bunch of "*STIFFS*"

1. Your boss is an "*IDIOT*"

Overwhelmingly, the number one reason that I have found for worker's discontent, is their inability to get along with their boss!

Which of the above reasons contributes most to your level of unhappiness and discontent at work? Think about this—if you had your own business, would any of these apply?

As a business-ownership advocate, I hope that if the last chapter did not convince you of the many benefits of starting your own business, then this chapter will. To those of you already in business and who are struggling, I hope this message reinforces your decision to keep moving forward despite all challenges that you are facing.

MY FAMILY

My wife's grandfather used to say this:

"Don't spend all your time making a living, that you fail to make a life!"

He was right—but keeping your family financially secure can be a big challenge. It doesn't happen automatically, as you can see from my story.

I graduated from the University of Montana in June of 1991, three and a half years after transferring from Albion College half-way through my freshman year because of my back injury.

One of my goals when I started college was that, no matter what, I would get my degree in four years. For those of you reading this book who are just starting college, or will be starting soon, I challenge you to do the same. Why? Because there are many benefits in doing so, such as:

- You will end up getting one to two more years of work experience than those on the I'll-get-my-degree-in-six-years plan.

- You'll save significantly on tuition ($10,000 and up).

- You could make $25,000-$30,000 with your first job out of college.

- Combined, the two previous points give you a net positive cash flow of almost $40,000 or more.

- You can begin earlier getting on solid financial footing to buy a house or start a family.

How can you accomplish this goal, when most institutions today state that college is a five- or six-year plan? They obviously adhere to the *Tommy Boy* belief system—a six-year game plan to graduate from college (*Tommy Boy*, the movie starring Chris Farley, is one of my all-time favorite comedies). I suggest the following:

- Take a minimum of four to five classes each semester.

- Treat your studies like a job, i.e., put in eight to nine hours a day.

- Take all morning classes (between 8 a.m. and noon), then after lunch each day study in the library until 5 p.m. This will free up your evenings and weekends to work or do whatever you would like.

If you have already graduated from college, teach this strategy to your children—it could save you both a lot of time and money!

I am proud to say that I have followed this course of action, and my family and I (ultimately the people for whom I work) have benefited tremendously due to my graduating in four years. My wife and I were blessed with our first child (Sam) when I was 22 years old. Had it not been for my graduating in four years and already having a full-time job, I would have had an even more difficult time supporting our young family.

During my senior year at U of M, I found a job doing marketing and advertising for the largest travel agency in Montana. I also spent a lot of time delivering tickets to their corporate accounts and changing the "day's specials" sign passers-by could see. I was treated like an errand boy by everyone except the general manager, Tom Schmidt, but I didn't let this get to me. Why? Because I knew that this position was only temporary, that I would soon be able to move onto something bigger and better.

My wife and I wanted to move to Seattle, so I began writing letters and sending resumes to companies in and around Seattle. Finally, I landed a job interview with a subsidiary of Holland America Cruise Lines' marketing division (Grayline Tours).

It was a cold and rainy Seattle day (imagine that) in December 1991 when I flew to Seattle for my interview. I landed that morning about 9 a.m. and had a return flight at 3:30 p.m. I went downtown, had the interview, and was offered a temporary six-month entry-level marketing position at $8 per hour, with no benefits. After six months my performance would be evaluated and only then would I be offered a full-time job (if my performance was satisfactory, of course). I wasn't thrilled with the offer, to say the least, but I accepted it because it was better than nothing.

So I walked outside in the cold Seattle rain. It was noon; I still had three hours before my return flight. But I didn't go to the airport. I was, as motivational speaker Les Brown says, HUNGRY and determined to find something better, so I scanned the Seattle skyline looking for the tallest skyscraper I could see. I spotted the Washington Mutual Tower building, drove there, then began on the top floor—the 54th—and went office to office handing out my resumes.

Most people quickly shoved me (figuratively speaking) back out the door, but I kept on because I was determined to find a better job offer. After more than an hour I finally landed in the office of Mutual Travel on the 18th floor. I walked in knowing something good was going to happen because I was already working for a travel agency. I told the receptionist that I didn't have an appointment but it was urgent that I speak with the Vice President of Sales because I knew that sales was my calling.

Well, to my surprise (and I think the receptionist's, too) out came the VP of Sales, who told me that I had five minutes to tell my story. Five minutes! Well, 30 minutes later I was offered a position in the Group Department until the next sales position came open. The Group Department position was permanent, full-time, with benefits and a starting salary of $18,000 per year. I know this isn't a lot of money by today's standards, but in 1991 it was decent money. I wasn't Bill Gates, but I had certainly done better than the temporary job at Holland America!

In late December of 1991, my wife and I moved to Seattle, and I began my new job with Mutual Travel. But I soon learned that $18,000 per year didn't go very far with a young family. After six months in the Group Department I was promoted to sales, but still was only making $22,000 per year.

To help our family, I took a second job delivering morning newspapers for the *Journal American*. It was pure hell throwing newspapers from 4:30 a.m. to 7 a.m. seven days a week just to make an extra $500 per month. However, I remembered who I worked for—MY FAMILY—and I kept on.

<u>The point of all this is that sometimes a person has to do something difficult or tiring to help their family. But most of the time these difficulties are only temporary—better times and better opportunities do come.</u>

When I worked two jobs, I also learned that not only is it important to try to maximize your income, but to also watch your spending habits as well. In the book *The Millionaire Next Door* written by Thomas Stanley and William Danko, I learned that:

"It doesn't matter how much money you make, but how much money you spend!"

It's equally important, in other words, to lessen your expenses as it is to earn more money!

EXERCISE

Very quickly, think of and list 10 ways you can immediately begin spending *less* money.

1.

2.

3.

4.

5.

6.

7

8.

9.

10.

MOVING UP

After nine months doing the paper route, I realized that what I needed was one better-paying job, not two lesser-paying jobs!

So I soon left Mutual Travel (and the paper route) to accept a sales position with Airborne Express. However, before

I left Mutual Travel, because of my Japanese language skills, I had the opportunity to hand deliver over 1,000 airline tickets to Japanese foreign exchange students who were to visit the United States later that summer. Each ticket was valued at more than $1,000. Therefore, at 23 years old I was sent to Tokyo (via business class) for five days, carrying a large duffle bag stuffed with over one million dollars worth of airline tickets. Let me tell you, I was a bit nervous going through Japanese customs, and very thankful to get through without a hitch. It was a tremendous experience!

Airborne Express (now a part of DHL) supplied me with a company car and an annual salary around $30,000. It was a great learning experience, although my wife and I still weren't able to dig out of our financial challenges. Why? Well, I also quickly learned that the more money you make, the more you spend! Remember what Confucius once said:

"When prosperity comes, do not use all of it."

I strongly believe that people cannot pursue their destiny if they first do not have their financial life in order. In Chapter Four we discussed creating multiple streams of income. It's also imperative to keep your spending habits in check. If you can successfully limit your spending, you'll be free—from a financial point of view—to pursue whatever it is that your heart desires!

At Airborne I had the opportunity to relocate and go into sales management, but I refused because my family and I—again, the people I work for—wanted to stay in Seattle, and moving up into sales management would've meant being transferred to somewhere like Spokane, Washington, or Boise, Idaho, or Grand Rapids, Michigan. These are all nice places to live, I'm sure—

but we wanted to stay in Seattle, plus with my wife's Washington legal education, it simply didn't make sense to move out of state. This decision reminds me of John Atkinson's quote:

"If you don't run your own life, somebody else will."

Therefore, after almost three years, I left Airborne and accepted a corporate sales position with Avis Rent-A-Car. Here's where I learned another important financial lesson. After I worked there for almost two years, the company was acquired. I had little stock in their company stock ownership plan (also called an ESOP)—I had nothing, in fact, except my old pay stubs!

But the company had a lot—they had the million-dollar accounts that I had brought to Avis. Even today, the revenue from my work continues to flow into Avis. Talk about residual income—most large corporations have this Wealth-Creation Principle mastered!

In my next job hunt, I ended up at a printed circuit board manufacturer in high-tech sales. The lesson I learned was that if you don't already own your own business, you need to work somewhere where you have the ability to become a part owner. After three years with two different circuit board companies, I finally had learned of an opportunity to receive a small ownership position in the form of stock options with Merix Corporation, a publicly traded company on NASDAQ. This company had given me what Ivey Stoke's wealth-creation principles taught me that I needed if I were to become wealthy—stock ownership. Because of my income-diversity philosophy, in addition to my business I intend to stay in sales for years to come. In fact, I encourage anyone who is working at their job for income, but pursuing their dream on the side during evenings and weekends, to continue with their day job *until it gets in the way of their dreams*. What I mean by this is that, eventually due to the proper execution of your game plan, you will start to make the lion's share of your income from your own business. When this begins to happen (be it one year from now or 10 years from now), then you can begin the transition from a day job to your own business opportunity. Two other factors to consider before you make this transition are, whether or not you have a year's worth of income saved, and if you are debt-free. I believe you need to have both of these things before you can make the switch.

From 1996 to 2001, during the early mornings, late evenings, and weekends, I wrote the first edition of this book while continuing to develop my speaking business on a part-time basis and working my day job full-time. By executing toward my passions and true destiny in life, I have continued to realize my lifetime goals — even though our family has been through the financial ups and downs involved with pursuing this destiny.

Looking back at all of our struggles, I can say with no regrets that it was well worth the financial rewards that we have realized as a result of following my dreams! My faith in God ultimately gave me the strength to continue pushing forward at a time when all the odds were stacked against me!

<u>Without question you, too, will be financially and emotionally tested on your way to achieving your destiny. If the belief in your vision is strong enough, you, too, will overcome every obstacle that gets in your way</u>!

Some of you reading this book may be questioning my loyalty—working for nine different companies over a period of 15 years. I see it this way:

My loyalty and faithfulness belong to MY FAMILY, and NOT a company!

If you desire to get ahead in corporate America, you need to look for a new job, at a minimum, every two to three years, and each job transition should pay you at least 20 percent more than your current salary. How else do you think I went from making just under $20,000 a year to over six figures in approximately 10 years? If you don't look for and take new jobs this often, you will continue to receive the standard five percent raise each year at review time. If you desire to make six figures, one way to do this—other than to own your own company—is to change jobs frequently.

The time to look for a new job is when you don't need one. That's when you can be selective.

However, if you wait until you have been laid off, and then begin looking, you will have far fewer options. You may, in fact, have to accept *less* money out of pure desperation.

One important thing to understand is that all companies are in business to make money (unless they're a non-profit organization). Therefore, most companies are going to pay you only enough to keep you from quitting! Consequently, because of this, many companies don't understand why many of their employees only work hard enough to keep from getting fired.

The only way to get paid what you're really worth, is to OWN your own business!

Many times, it may take owning and learning from several businesses before you find your "pot of gold." I have learned many things from at least half a dozen business opportunities that I have owned over the years. I have then taken these important lessons from each endeavor into the next opportunity, and have benefited from all of them in one way or another. As I stated earlier, just because your old 'beater' of a car failed on you at one time or another and left you stranded on the side of the road, you didn't give up on driving and spend the rest of your life walking. You simply got yourself another car and tried again. The same concept holds true with owning a business.

If you are content with your annual five percent raises, then ALL you are doing for yourself and your family is giving you the ability to now order out for pizza one more time per each pay period. That's it! There isn't much left over from a five percent pay raise after taxes. Just based on the fact that you are reading this book tells me that you WILL NOT be content with only five percent, and that you will DEMAND more from yourself!

You simply need to understand that moving on to a new company is NOT an emotional decision (emotional decisions should only be made in the field of "love"—who you will marry, etc.). All other decisions, especially career and financial decisions, should be based on facts and "accurate thinking"! Napoleon Hill understood this well when he said:

"The single greatest trait of successful people, is the process of accurate thinking."

See, moving on to a new company or opportunity (including starting your own business) is simply a business decision based on facts. You can and will make new friends wherever you go, and your old friends will stick with you if they are truly "good friends!"

You may be asking yourself, *How do I find a better job if I don't have the free time to pursue what I want?* The answer is to let other people take you to these opportunities. Remember when we talked about asset leveraging in the previous chapter? Simply put, have others work for you to help you uncover these hidden opportunities. Get a recruiter of one kind or another to start working for you. Never pay the recruiter to do so (unless you are seeking your first job out of college). Almost all recruiters are paid by the company who is looking for qualified applicants. I have worked with recruiters on two different occasions, and in both instances I was offered a job and accepted the position, both of which were at a salary much higher than what I was previously making.

I have a tremendous amount of respect and gratitude to a large national recruiting company called Management Recruiters International (MRI). Jim Kozich of MRI placed me in my most lucrative position to date in high-tech sales. Although I personally haven't used the large national Internet recruiting companies, such as hotjobs.com, monster.com, or thingamajob.com, if I were looking to make a move now, I would definitely check these out. Another option is to network with people in your industry as often as possible, as well as to regularly attend job fairs and job expos. Lastly, please make certain that you get someone to help you (even if you have to pay for it) put together a winning resume!

If you are not interested in owning your own business (for whatever reason) and enjoy the excitement of corporate America, I simply urge you to make certain that the corporate ladder that you are climbing is not leaning against the wrong wall!

THE CHALLENGES NEVER END

The problem with many working people today is that they feel that job security is attainable. Once they have a job, most people think their career challenges are over. This is false:

Job security NO LONGER EXISTS.

In today's new high-tech world, companies are facing even greater challenges to remain competitive. These companies will do anything to build the bottom line, including laying off people. The funny thing is that they don't say that they are FIRING you, they say you are being LAID OFF, i.e., you just happen to be one of the unfortunate ones. With the recession in late 2000 and 2001, I've personally known literally hundreds of people who have been laid off, including myself!

Unfortunately I too was a victim of corporate downsizing in September 2001. Eight days after the September 11th tragedy (and after almost three years of a successful sales record), I was laid off by Merix. Thankfully, I was given an attractive severance package and was also able to get another sales position within two weeks with a competitor in the PCB industry called TTM Technologies. This experience of being laid off was very difficult for me, but through this adversity, I learned the truth of what Nietzche once said:

"That which does not kill, STRENGTHENS!"

After 18 months at TTM Technologies, I was transitioned to a commission only manufacturer's representative due to market conditions in the printed circuit board industry. It was kind of like being laid off, because I lost my entire salary. As a result, I sold circuit boards very much on a part-time basis. This gave me a chance to go full time with my own business. I realized that I needed to diversify my business by offering speaking and publishing coaching help to others. My clients are now thrilled that I can assist them in becoming published. I have also helped many others evolve from "free speaking" to "fee speaking." If you or someone you know needs these services, please have them contact me. To learn more, visit my web site and then click on "**Publishing Help**."

I have also created business opportunities for readers who have asked if they can help me market this book. I have created a "Destiny Achievers Club" where anyone can create a part-time business by purchasing 100 books at a discounted price, then selling them at full retail price to earn extra income. These club members can also earn commissions when booking me to speak. To learn more, visit my web site and click on "**Biz Opportunity**."

Getting back to layoffs, the problem is that when companies go through downsizing, the victims (including myself) have virtually NOTHING to show for their work except old paycheck stubs. Most simply look for another job, hoping that they can get hired (so that they can probably get slapped in the face again). This is foolish. Haven't these victims learned their lesson?

To combat this, I recommend that you do some soul-searching (as I have done) and turn your hobby into a home-based business. Now if you do happen to get laid off, at least you have a second alternative to fall back on.

<u>You owe it to yourself and your family to build something that becomes an asset, rather than just wasting time on a job renting out your skills!</u>

After my experience of being laid off, I made a decision to build my own business in such a way that I will NEVER again become fully dependent on a job to support my family. I have made a decision to become UNSTOPPABLE, and as a result, my own business has skyrocketed. Soon I will be able to retire from corporate America, when I am debt free and have one year's worth of income saved, so that I can build my own business full time. When this happens, I will be in complete control of my own destiny! If you truly want to create your own destiny, I encourage you to start your own business and do the same (but make certain you have a year's worth of income saved before you leave your job).

LEARNING TO FISH

My experience over time of basically getting laid off from two companies in 18 months has taught me the true meaning of an old fish story that I am sure you have heard at one point or another. It goes like this:

Give a man a fish and he eats for a day. But teach a man HOW to fish and he will eat for a lifetime!

See, having a job is just like getting a fish (your paycheck) given to you every other Friday. This is ultimately how you eat. When you get laid off and loose your paycheck, you starve! The key then is to learn HOW to fish (how to earn money in a business you own). Then, as a result, you can fish whenever and wherever you want and eat as much as you want (earn as much as you desire), as often as you want.

I never really liked fishing as a kid because I rarely caught anything (even though I enjoyed all the time I spent with my Dad listening to his stories). However, I absolutely love fishing for income as an adult because of the freedom it allows. If you want more freedom in life, you must learn HOW to fish for yourself!

There is absolutely NOTHING wrong with having a job because it allows you to eat. But make certain that while you are eating at the job, you work on your dream on the side and learn how to fish for yourself.

ENSLAVEMENT TO YOUR EMPLOYER

In talking about being able to provide for your family, or relying upon someone else (your employer) to provide your fish, reminds me of this issue: Are we really free given this "work like mad environment" of the new millennium? At the beginning of this book one of the questions that I asked you was: Are you free?

The reason that I pose this question is that many people believe that slavery ended on January 1, 1863 when President Abraham Lincoln signed the *Emancipation Proclamation*. However, I believe that as long as we have a job we are enslaved to our employers and are NOT truly free!

Given the fact that all workers are given a limited amount of income in return for working fifty weeks (out of fifty-two weeks per year) to earn their pay, it becomes obvious to me that employees are not as free as some may think.

If you disagree with this belief, let me pose you a few questions. Why is it that employees must ask permission from their employers to go on an extended vacation, when business owners can go on vacation any time they desire (for as long as they want) without having to ask permission from anyone to do so?

The kind of slavery that existed in the 1800s in America has gratefully ended largely in part due to the efforts of President Lincoln, but a different kind of enslavement exists today with our employers!

Some of you may be thinking that a six month vacation is not really practical. Well then, how about on any given hot summer day, can you just take the day off from work and go to the beach together as a family? Or do you and your spouse need to ask permission from your employers to spend this day together as a family?

As a business owner, you will become FREE and NEVER again have to ask for permission to spend quality time together with your family!

In talking about freedom and enslavement to an employer while giving speeches on this topic, I have been both ridiculed and admired at the same time. The ridicule has come from employees who still believe in job security and that their employer will take care of all of their financial needs in the future. However, at the same time I have been admired and given an overwhelmingly stamp of approval from business owners because they flourish in their freedom and absolutely love spending extra time with their family.

A job is a GOOD thing but you must realize that it is nothing more than a temporary vehicle to pay your bills and support your family while you are building your dream.

Being enslaved to an employer is acceptable only if you are building your long term vehicle of business ownership in a field in which you have passion.

Business Opportunities

When thinking about this controversial subject, always remember what was mentioned in the last chapter. 90 percent of the wealth is owned by only 10 percent of the people. These 10 percent of the people are the business owners, the remaining folks are employees. Which side of the equation do you want to find yourself?

The following exercises are designed to help you sort through your ideas and all the various options that you are faced with in today's business environment. Remember, there are a million ways to make a million dollars—you just have to execute in one way! Follow your heart, and it will make the choice for you!

Exercise A

Sit quietly for at least 10 minutes. Then write in the space that follows five business opportunities you've come up with (or have been exposed to) that can generate additional streams of income for your family. Think of hobbies that you could turn into businesses. Remember that a home-based business provides more tax benefits. Also, remember that whatever business you choose, it must be consistent with your values and goals:

1.

2.

3.

4.

5.

EXERCISE B

If you don't feel that you can own or run a business, or have the desire to, then list some companies / organizations for which you desire to work (also list job titles). You should make certain that they are very <u>stable</u> and are <u>capable</u> of helping you attain your long-term goals:

1.

2.

3.

4.

5.

EXERCISE C

List five actions that you can take immediately to help turn either of the two previous exercises into a reality:

1.

2.

3.

4.

5.

When starting a business, you need to align your passions with an opportunity that you can do from home. This will give you the ability to be there for you family. Try and shy away from any business in which you must "lock and unlock" daily, unless this kind of business is your passion. Try and build a business where you can earn income without having employees, or having to be there all of the time (you don't want to create a prison for yourself). I have worked from home now for almost ten years. I can't even imagine going back to a daily commute. Because I work from home, I am better able to meet the needs of my family. If you also worked from home, could you better meet your family's needs?

SUMMARY

Your boss is you and your family! This is a secret that most people never learn. One reason why there are so many broken families is because too many people place more importance on their job than on their family.

Your business card may read "ABC Company," but your heart should say, "Your Family"!

I know this sounds difficult. We are all challenged to try to make it financially while also being there for our families. It's difficult to balance both. Sometimes you'll fail. But when you do, you must simply try again. I believe that failure isn't final, instead failure teaches us lessons. And we all want to learn more, right? The more we fail, the more we learn. It was Henry Ford who summed up this principle when he said:

"Failure is only the opportunity to more intelligently begin again."

In addition to Henry Ford, Thomas Edison has failed on more than a few occasions. In fact over the course of his life (1847-1931), Thomas Edison failed thousands of times while following his passion of inventing new things capable of changing the world. As a result in 1879, he produced the first *reliable*, long-lasting source of light with his incandescent light bulb. Below is a quote from Thomas Edison regarding his view on using the knowledge learned from past failures to move forward:

"Unfortunately, many of life's failures are experienced by people who did not realize how close they were to success when they gave up. If I find 10,000 ways something won't work, I haven't failed because every wrong attempt discarded is just one more step forward!"

It's so important to understand this. If you still have difficulty with this, I suggest you read the book *Failing Forward* by John C. Maxwell. It's a must-read for understanding this concept.

As I stated earlier, no one ever ends up on their death bed wishing that they would have spent more time at the office, but many wish they would have spent more time with their children, spouse, and loved ones. These are, after all, the people you work for—not the people at your place of employment!

I challenge you to spend twice as much time with your children, and half as much money. There is an old saying that goes like this:

"Children are like a bank. The more time you put in with them, the greater the return will be on your investment of time."

Also, always remember what Dr. Robert Brooks says about the importance of being there for our children:

"One of the most important factors that contributes to the resilience in children is the presence of at least one person in their lives who believes in them!"

The late psychologist Julius Segal says that this person is a "charismatic adult," a person from whom children "gather strength." I challenge you to be "that person" in someone's life in your community!

Please remember that our children are, after all, the future of this world. If you don't really believe that it's important to spend a lot of time with your children, then please watch the movie "Traffic" starring Michael Douglas. His character, Bob Wakefield, almost lost his daughter to a life of drugs on the streets, simply because he was too busy and selfish building his career to spend quality time with her.

<u>I challenge you to never forget for whom you really work…your family, your children, and yourself. Put your family ahead of your work and you will experience more <u>*love*</u> and more <u>*happiness*</u> in life</u>!

As in the case of the MasterCard® example used at the beginning of this chapter, I also know for whom I work! For this same reason, I am proud to say that the footprints that appear in the sand on this book's front cover, are that of my children! This is just one photo from the many family vacations we have taken in Hawaii.

CHAPTER 6

Conquering Adversity, Temptation, & Addiction

"My advantage is that I can endure more pain than anyone else in the world!"
— Steve Prefontaine

To reach your life's destiny and to achieve more *love* and more *health*, you will need to eliminate all excuses and reasons not to do something in your life. You'll also need to overcome addiction and adversity—one (the addictions) you can control, the other (the adversity) you often *can't control*. Additionally you will need to gain control over your temptations. But if you are a person who can beat adversity, temptation, and addiction and who also stays true to your core values and beliefs, then nothing will stop you!

Let me tell you about an experience that presented my family and I with a great deal of adversity—so much so we almost lost our lives! What's more, this adversity was the result of someone else's addiction!

On the evening of May 29, 1982, at 10:53 p.m., my parents and one of my sisters were in their upstairs bedrooms sleeping. My parents had spent almost every free moment of the previous week preparing for my oldest sister Margaret's high school graduation party, which would take place the next day. My brother Tim, cousin Tom, and I were watching a movie in the family room when all of a sudden we heard a loud roar of a truck scream around the corner of our street going way too fast. Then we heard dirt and rocks scatter as this truck turned down the gravel road next to our house. Then—again, with no additional warning—we felt the house shudder as the truck hit our house at a terrible speed!

I ran into the living room to see the damage. The truck had smashed into the foundation of our house and in doing so, the truck pushed our gas meter into our basement's foundation. Every window on the west side of the house was engulfed in bright orange flames. I ran out of the house screaming, "Fire! Fire!" and everyone followed out the front door.

A neighbor across the street had witnessed the accident and called the fire department. Our family stood outside and watched our house burn. The truck driver—who, it turned out later, was driving drunk—had driven directly into the side of our house at about 40 mph and had hit our gas meter dead on center. The heat from his engine and the crash ignited the natural gas line, which had been broken upon impact.

Although the fire department and police arrived quickly, the gas line was buried beneath the road so the fire department couldn't turn off the gas. Our house burned until 12:30 a.m. One side of our two-story home had burned.

During this time, our family, along with about 50 other curious people, stood watching the fire in shock and horror.

The driver of the truck, who at first ran away and then returned only after my cousin chased him down, stood in the yard screaming at my mother, "Save my truck! Save my truck!" Being drunk, he actually put his arm around my mother's shoulder—she was standing there in her nightgown—and he started shaking her. I stepped between them just as the officer grabbed this man to escort him to the police car. To this day I can vividly remember the drunken stench from the man and the intense heat of the fire!

When the fire was finally put out, we stood huddled in our yard together. I'll never forget my mother's words to us:

<u>"Everything will be fine, because no one has died and we're all safely together!"</u>

Now realize that when my mother, Lois Snow, said this, we:

- Did not have a place to sleep
- Did not have any clothes or personal items
- Did not have any food

The fire and smoke damage had ruined everything, but my mother was fine. Sure, she was shaken, just like we were; but she focused not on the adversity we had faced or would face in the weeks and months ahead. Instead, she focused on the fact that we were *all* safe and alive! I strongly believe that my character was forever formed by that moment, that my tendency to always be optimistic in life now was greatly influenced by my mother that day and her ability to see our cup as "half full," not "half empty."

Needless to say, having a major house fire was not a one-day problem. That night we slept on the floor of the church across the street. The next morning we returned to our home. The Fire Marshal, investigating the accident, told us that we were all lucky to be alive. The gas meter, he explained, had been pushed into the basement wall, but thankfully there had been a small gap to allow the gas to escape. Had the meter been pushed into the basement an additional half inch, he said, the house would have immediately exploded into a ball of fire and we would have all, more than likely, perished.

We *were* lucky to be alive! See, our family got a second chance on life! I believe that with each passing day, all of us get a "second chance" because tomorrows are NOT promised (as we have learned from the tragedies of September 11th). The question that I want to pose to you is this:

What are you going to do each and every day with your *second chance on life*?

LIFE LESSONS

All of us will face adversity in our lives. It's part of life. The adversity may not be as scary as having a house fire, or being a family victim of the September 11th tragedies, but the challenges toward your destiny can be just as severe. Watching my parents deal with, and overcome, the adversity of our house fire showed me the importance of a positive attitude.

My mother didn't focus or dwell on what had happened, the negative; she focused on the positive. This strong character served her again years later, when she successfully battled and overcame breast cancer.

Exercise

Think of a time when you faced a serious physical adversity, such as an accident or major illness.

What fears did you face at the time?

_____

_____

_____

_____

_____

What factors helped you overcome this adversity?

_____

_____

_____

_____

_____

What lessons or beliefs did this adversity bring forth that you still use today?

_____

_____

_____

_____

_____

OVERCOMING ADVERSITY

The following are some specific ways I recommend to both anticipate adversities and to overcome them when they do in fact enter your life.

- Understand that adversities are only temporary (better times are bound to come). Nothing lasts forever, in other words. Focus as much as possible on solutions rather than the negative aspects of the adversity.

- Appreciate all that is good in your life. Even when something bad happens, you still will have many positive things to draw on: your health, family, children, freedom, etc.

- Remember those people before you who have persevered when faced with more difficult times (Holocaust survivors, victims of war, POWs, etc.).

- Know deep down in your heart that you have what it takes to persevere. You can face and overcome adversities. You've done it before, you'll do it again.

- Understand that when one door closes, another almost always opens up. Look for "hidden opportunities" when faced with an adversity; something positive is almost always lurking close behind.

DEALING WITH TEMPTATION

As we slowly overcome adversity, oftentimes we fall victim to our own temptations. Then, once we bow down to temptation, oftentimes it gets the better of us and we start making the same mistakes over and over again. If we fall into this trap, life's temptations can literally steal years of time away from our already short lives. This reality reminds me of David Norris' quote on time:

> **"How you spend your time is more important than how you spend your money. Money mistakes can be corrected, but time is gone forever."**

I have found a powerful poem from an unknown source on the Internet which I believe best describes how our minds work with regards to temptation.

WOLVES

An old Cherokee is teaching his grandson about life.

"A fight is going on inside me," he said to the boy. "It is a terrible fight and it is between two wolves.

One is evil—he is anger, envy, sorrow, regret, greed, arrogance, self-pity, guilt, resentment, inferiority, lies, false pride, superiority, and ego.

The other is good—he is joy, peace, love, hope, serenity, humility, kindness, benevolence, empathy, generosity, truth, compassion, and faith.

This same fight is going on inside you, and inside every other person, too."

The grandson thought about it for a minute and then asked his grandfather, "Which wolf will win?"

The old Cherokee simply replied, "The one you feed."

I challenge you to feed only the good wolf! If you do so, you will be able to overcome adversity, temptation, and addictions. As a result, your mind will be free to follow your heart and create your own destiny in life!

THE HORROR OF ADDICTIONS

Having our home burn was an adversity my entire family had to overcome. But closely linked to why our house burned was the reason—a drunken driver!

I was 13 years old when this event happened. While 13 is relatively young, I was still able to see what alcohol abuse can do to a society in general and individuals in particular. That night, May 29, 1982, I committed myself to a principle that I am proud to say I've always lived by: to never ever get drunk; in fact, I refuse to drink alcohol period!

I saw firsthand what alcohol can do to a person. I've seen in others the fear that develops when alcohol takes control of their life. Because of this experience, I am proud to state that I AM A MAN OF MY WORD AND PRINCIPLES—to this day I still do not drink!

Don't get me wrong: I don't believe drinking alcohol is wrong. I am certain that drinking AND driving is dead wrong! But for me, I still choose not to drink. My friends and others have sometimes made fun of me for this, but I'm okay with it, because no amount of ridicule will ever change my core principles!

Remember this old saying:

**"If you don't stand for something,
you'll fall for anything!"**

What your addiction is doesn't matter: it may be alcohol, nicotine, overeating, drugs, pornography, or a hundred other things that, when abused, can harm you and others. If not conquered, these addictions will take control of you, they will beat you down, they will stop you from reaching your destiny! In fact, it was Epictetus who once said:

"No man is free who is not a master of himself."

EXERCISE

What addictions (or similar "bad habits") are there in your life that you'd like to stop doing?

_____

_____

_____

_____

_____

Up to this point, what has stopped you from stopping?

_____

_____

_____

_____

What steps can you begin to take *today* to stop your addiction or bad habit?

_____

_____

_____

_____

_____

Over consumption of alcohol and other substances are bad for your health. As noted speaker and author Zig Ziglar says, if you owned a million-dollar race horse, you wouldn't let it stay up nights boozin', smoking, and drinking coffee like there's no tomorrow, would you? Absolutely not! So why would we treat our own bodies this way?

HOW TO CONQUER ADDICTIONS

I know—it's easy to *say* don't do something, but actually not *doing* it is much harder. I realize that. Here are ways I suggest that you utilize to help you conquer your addictions.

- Acknowledge the fact that you have a problem. Often this is a relief to people—they don't have to "hide" or otherwise "pretend" any longer.

- Ask yourself this question: *What will likely happen to me if I don't conquer this addiction over time?* Will you damage your health? Could you possibly be charged with a crime? Would it cause embarrassment or other problems for your family? Could you lose your job?

- Seek out professional help. Everyone needs help at some point, especially dealing with a long-held habit or addiction.

- Live one day at a time. Don't expect to be perfect from the outset. Just as a habit or addiction "took hold" over time, it will take a certain amount of time to stop.

- Focus daily on your life-long goals. Again, this will help you focus on something positive in your life, a point in the future which you can move toward.

As a result of conquering your addictions, you will ultimately get two things that most everyone wants—more *health* and more *love!*

THE POWER OF A POSITIVE ATTITUDE

Many people have asked me a variation on this question: "Patrick, I'm struggling to conquer my addictions and adversities, but it's difficult to do so and keep a positive attitude. How do I stay positive during these difficult times?"

That's a good question. It's also an important one, because only those who can conquer adversity and overcome addictions will achieve their destiny. One thing I suggest to my audiences is to try to never get discouraged. You will face challenges—that's part of life—but don't let them beat you. Instead, focus on the big picture, on all the many things that you have to be thankful for. Franklin Deleanor Roosevelt once said:

"When you come to the end of your rope, tie a knot and hang on."

Here's an example of someone who always focused on what's positive in his life. A few years ago, when I was making a sales call on Intel, I met a patriotic veteran named Ron Dyer. He had two small American flags in his office as a show of his patriotism. I asked Ron to share with me some of his life philosophies. He said that because he had done multiple tours of duty in Vietnam and that his life was at stake dozens of times, he now was able to keep things in perspective. Ron Dyer then said,

"Every day that goes by in which I am NOT shot at, is a good day, regardless of what else happens to me!"

How's that for a life philosophy? I think this is a good quote for all of us to learn how to overcome the many daily adversities we all face—to keep our problems in perspective! When life gets you down, focus instead on what you have, what you can be grateful for! I challenge you to start each day in the shower mentally reviewing all the positive things in your life.

Don't celebrate Thanksgiving only once a year—why not count your blessings every day?

If you are still challenged to find the good in life and acknowledge all that you are blessed with, I encourage you to read this poem from an unknown "Ed." It is filled with statistics on how good we really have it in life. If these stats are even halfway true, then we have little, if anything to be depressed about!

GIVING THANKS

If you woke up this morning with more health than illness, you are more blessed than the million who will not survive this week.

If you have never experienced the danger of battle, the loneliness of imprisonment, and agony of torture, or the pangs of starvation, you are ahead of 500 million people in the world.

If you can attend a church meeting without fear of harassment, arrest, torture, or death, you are more blessed than 3 billion people in the world.

If you have food in the refrigerator, clothes on your back a roof overhead and a place to sleep, you are richer than 75 percent of this world.

If you have money in the bank, in your wallet, and spare change in a dish someplace, you are among the top 8 percent of the world's wealthy.

If your parents are still alive and still married, you are very rare, even in the United States.

If you hold up your head with a smile on your face and are truly thankful, you are blessed because the majority can, but most do not.

If you can hold someone's hand, hug them, or even touch them on the shoulder, you are blessed because you can offer healing touch.

If you can read this message, you just received a double blessing in that someone was thinking of you, and furthermore, you are more blessed than over 2 billion people in the world who cannot read at all.

Have a good day, count your blessings, and pass this along to remind everyone else how blessed we all are.

EXERCISE

Spend a few minutes thinking about all that you have to be thankful for, then list as many as you can in the space provided. Refer to this page later when you're feeling particularly "down."

_____

_____

_____

_____

_____

_____

Now write out all the things that you are grateful for in your life that you may LOSE if you do NOT overcome your addictions:

_____

_____

_____

_____

_____

_____

_____

SUMMARY

There's no question that you WILL face many adversities in your life, both large and small. You may also have addictions or other "bad habits" that are holding you back from reaching your goals. Occasionally, we will all give in to one sort of temptation or another. But only the people who are prepared to FACE and then OVERCOME adversity, temptation, and addiction will reach their fullest potential.

Always try and think of what your future holds for you—you need to take responsibility for your actions! Never underestimate how wonderful and blessed you are to be in good health. You have a lot of things in life to be grateful for—don't take anything for granted.

A problem that many of us face today is that we enter the work force around age 20, in good health—then we spend the next 30 years earning money, only to lose our health in the process. Once our health is lost (after working for 30 years), we spend all the money that we have earned, trying simply to regain the health that we once had (prior to working). If you think about how true this really is, you will realize the value of *time* in our lives, since we all have an expiration date (time is precious—don't waste it). If you want more *health* in your life, my challenge is this: Don't let adversity, temptation, addiction, or making a living rob you of your health! Health is always more important than money—just ask someone who has lost their health but still has money.

When faced with a challenge in your life, refer specifically to this chapter. Don't get caught up in self-pity; *you can and will overcome anything that life presents to you.* As you overcome these challenges, you will certainly experience more *health* and more *love* as a result!

CHAPTER 7

Overcoming Your Fears

"Once a man has made a commitment to a way of life, he puts the greatest strength in the world behind him. It's something we call heart power. Once a man has made this commitment, nothing can stop him short of success."

— Vince Lombardi

In the last three chapters, we've talked a great deal about creating a firm financial footing, putting family ahead of work, and conquering adversity, temptation, and addiction. Now is the time to begin implementing your "next steps" and go! In other words, let's let the fun begin!

But this also is the point where many people falter. Why? The planning and preparing are behind them; action must now be taken. But to take action can be—to many people—scary. Their fears are often so strong and compelling that their actions are ineffective—if they take any action at all. It was author David Joseph Schwartz who said:

"Do what you fear and the fear disappears."

I use several sayings to help me remember the importance of taking action, all of which help me overcome fear:

Taking actions overcome your fears
Action equals results
This year's efforts, pay next year's bills
Today's work will fund tomorrow's
biggest dreams

Author and speaker Les Brown has said that:

"You are currently molding your future; whatever you are now doing will result in what your future holds for you."

I believe that what Les Brown says about taking action is one of the ultimate truths in life. Here's another way to look at the concept of taking action. I have saved the following excerpt from Murray McBride's forum for many years because I believe it emphasizes how important taking action is, especially when put in the context of fear:

"Every morning in Africa, a gazelle wakes up. It knows it must out-run the fastest lion or it will be killed.

Every morning in Africa, a lion wakes up. It knows it must out-run the slowest gazelle or it will starve.

It doesn't matter whether you're a lion or a gazelle: WHEN THE SUN COMES UP, YOU'D BETTER BE RUNNING!"

EXERCISE

Think back to a time when you were ready to begin a big project, such as starting your own business or taking an important personal action, such as moving to a new city.

Did fear arise? _____

_____

_____

_____

How so? _____

_____

_____

_____

What did you do to lessen and, eventually, overcome this fear? _____

_____

_____

_____

What lessons about fear did this experience teach you?

_____

_____

_____

_____

EVERYONE HAS FEAR

One of the main things to remember when fear arises within you is this: everyone has fears! The key is to accept this fact and *still move forward despite your fears*. This, I believe, is the true meaning of courage!

If you feel confused and frightened before beginning something, think of Christopher Columbus in 1492. When he started, he didn't know where he was going. When he got there, he didn't know where he was. And when he returned to Spain, he didn't know where he had been. Plus he had made his great sailing voyages all on borrowed money!

Here's a more recent example. In my opinion, I don't think anyone in modern history has put their fears aside and gone out on a limb more than the late Dr. Martin Luther King. Dr. King concluded his last speech on April 3, 1968, in Memphis, Tennessee, with these words:

"Well, I don't know what will happen now; we've got some difficult times ahead. But it doesn't really matter with me now, because I have seen the mountaintop. And I don't mind. Like anybody, I would like to live a long life— longevity has its place. But I am not concerned about that now. I just want to do God's will. And He's allowed me to go up to the mountain. And I've looked over, and I've seen the promised land. And so I'm happy tonight: I'm not worried about anything; I'm fearing no man. Mine eyes have seen the glory of the coming of the Lord!"

We all know the tragic fate of Dr. King. What's important to remember is that he put his fear aside and did what his heart told him to do. And because of that, he is arguably one of the most important world leaders to have ever lived because of his human-rights accomplishments that reverberated around the globe!

Martin Luther King was an amazing man of God. I am certain that because of his faith he was better prepared to minimize his fears. Dr. King reminds me of Reverend Dick Gregory's quote:

"Fear and God do not occupy the same space!"

EXERCISE

Think for a moment, then list dreams or activities that you have thought about doing at some point but which you have never begun or completed because of fear or apprehension:

_____

_____

_____

Once you have listed these, circle the ones that you still have time to accomplish when you overcome your fears.

HOW TO PUT YOUR FEARS ASIDE

To succeed in life and reach your destiny, you must develop BELIEF and TRUST in yourself. It was French novelist Anatole France (1844-1924) who said:

"To accomplish great things we must not only act, but also dream not only plan, but also believe."

Only when you trust your abilities and believe in yourself, can you overcome your fears and leap into whatever it is that your heart is calling you to do. Here's a poem from an unknown author that I feel represents this point well:

> **The jump**
> **is so frightening**
> **between**
> **where I am,**
> **and where**
> **I want to be...**
> **Because of all**
> **I may become,**
> **I will close my eyes**
> **and leap!**

I know, I know—trusting yourself is easier said than done! Just like Columbus and Martin Luther King, however, you must learn to put your fears aside and then pursue what it is that you want to accomplish. Here are some specific ways I've found to reduce or eliminate fear. I call this my:

FEAR DESTRUCTION PROCESS

- Understand that you only live on Earth *one time.* Thus, you must make every moment count.

- Study the true risk of the situation at hand. How much fear is legitimate, and how much is simply a matter of your own mind?

- Ask yourself, "If I don't do this, then will it haunt me for the rest of my life?" Regret is one of the most disappointing and disheartening human emotions!

- Ask yourself, "is there something that I fear that must be overcome if I am to reach my goals?" Often, focusing on what we can obtain, such as goals, helps us reduce fear.

- Ask yourself, "Could the task at hand get me killed?" I know this sounds extreme, but it also helps put things in perspective.

Now I'm going to give you two examples in my life in which I had to overcome fear to really break through a barrier to accomplish my goals (one family related, the other career related).

My family travels to Maui every February and we stay at Kaanapali Beach. At the far north end of Kaanapali Beach, there's a huge rock / cliff formation that protrudes out into the ocean about a quarter of a mile. This area is also one of the best snorkeling spots in all of Maui, if not Hawaii. The cliff is called "Black Rock" and many of the local kids jump or dive off this 40- to 50-foot cliff for fun. Well, after watching this for several days, my son, Sam, who was nine at the time, decided that he and his father (that's me) were going to jump off this cliff into the ocean below. Later that day my wife overheard Sam telling some other kids at the resort's pool (where we were staying) what we were going to do. Well, to say the least, I hate jumping from high places, regardless of how deep the water is!

At this point, I realized that I'd never have shared with my son the story of the time I climbed up the headwall of Mount Washington (the highest mountain east of the Mississippi River). It was during the summer of 1981. I was 12 years old, and my sister and I went on a hiking vacation with some friends in the White Mountains of New Hampshire. At one point on this trip, my 13-year-old friend and I took a shortcut away from the others and soon found ourselves perched on the headwall of Mount Washington like two baby eagles in their nest. We were traversing the edge of a cliff on a trail about 12 inches wide and had to maneuver 100 feet to the other side to get to safety. This cliff, which had claimed many lives, dropped more than 1,000 feet straight down. I was scared to death since I could have easy fallen and lost my life. We safely made it to the other side going very slowly without the use of ropes. At that point in my life, I decided that NEVER again in my life would I ever find myself positioned at the top of a cliff—regardless of the circumstances!

Therefore, being presented with both the challenge of jumping off this cliff in Maui, and my son's questioning of my manliness, I found myself evaluating this potential jump from every angle. But here is what came to me:

- I realized that I only live once, and that I was, after all, on vacation.

- I studied the level of risk involved. I had seen many kids jump off that cliff, and no one had hit any rocks below. I even watched them enter the water from below the surface through my snorkel mask.

- I then asked myself, "If I don't do this, what will my son think of me?" Well, obviously he'd think that I'm a wimp. But I wanted him to view me as a *hero*…just as I view my own Dad (a golfer, who has made three holes-in-one in his lifetime!).

- If I am to be adventurous as one of my life goals indicates, then I should jump.

- Finally, I concluded that if I jumped out as far as I could, then I would certainly miss the side of the cliff and land in the water. (I may hit the water awfully hard, but I knew I would *live*!)

With this due diligence behind me, my son and I both jumped off Black Rock. In fact, we did it twice! Let me tell you, it was quite a rush! My wife took pictures of both of us in mid-air, and they turned out great! My son now thinks I am a "hero" for jumping, and we will share this incredible memory together forever! Now, I jump at least one time each and every year that we visit Maui.

The reason that I share this experience is to ask you:

What cliffs are you faced with in your life that you must jump from, to get from where you are now, to where you want to go?

Speaking of heroes, my wife and I have another wonderful son named Jacob. When he was a young child, we used to take him to the beach frequently to look for crabs under the rocks. He soon learned that the bigger the rocks were, the more crabs there would be hidden underneath. As a result, we turned over small rocks, then bigger rocks, then we somehow turned over even bigger rocks. As we did this, he would get more and more excited because he would see more crabs each time as the rocks got bigger. He then pointed to this huge boulder (almost the size of a minivan) and said,

"Dad, if you could pick up that rock, then you would be my hero!" I was not able to lift up that boulder, but I will always remember this moment that we shared together.

The question that I would like to ask you parents is this: What can you do in your life to become your child's hero? Understand that, in many cases, in order to become your child's hero you may need to overcome your fears.

Here's my career-related example about overcoming fear. I spent four years going back and forth as to whether or not I should hunker down and finish this book. I finally realized that the "true risk" to my career was to *not* follow through with what my heart had told me to do. My heart had told me that this book and my speaking career were my passions, and that if I were to be truly happy and fulfilled in life, then I *must* make this happen. If I hadn't listened to this internal message, two things could have happened:

- I could have spent the rest of my days regretting my lack of action (or inaction), and I'd always be disappointed in myself for not living up to my full potential.

- I'd be stuck with only a sales career and making a decent living—I'd be building, in other words, wealth for someone else instead of for me. I would then be questioning myself as to why I had limited my options to just "a job," when I could accomplish so much more.

It is only natural to let fear get in your way and to question yourself and wonder what others will think of you as you pursue your goals. Les Brown has said that you should:

"Never let someone else's opinion of you become your reality!"

Don't worry about what other people think of you and your aspirations. No one but you can measure the size and strength of your heart!

If your heart is telling you what your passion is, then follow it and great things will happen in your life; I'm confident of this!

PAIN AND PLEASURE

Putting your fears aside can be a very painful experience. I'll be the first to admit this fact, because I've known my share of pain! But pain can be a positive. Before I explain how, here's a quick story:

A mailman delivered the mail to an old man who sat on his porch with his dog. Every day the mailman would wonder why the dog was moaning. Finally the mailman asked the old man this question, and the old man replied, "There's a nail sticking up from the porch that's jabbing him in the side." The mailman said, "Well then, why doesn't your dog get up and move?" to which the old man replied, "Well, I guess it doesn't hurt him enough to make him move."

Many pains are like the one being faced by the dog: pains that are small and nagging but not strong enough to motivate us. Well-known speaker and motivational coach Anthony Robbins says that human motivations (actions) stem from two main sources: our desire to avoid pain or gain pleasure.

If you have something jabbing you in the side of life, don't be afraid, like the old dog, and simply sit there and keep moaning. I challenge you to get up and do something about your pain, and take the necessary action or actions to control your circumstances. I guarantee that if you do, you will be one step closer to creating your own destiny!

SUMMARY

Overcoming your fears is difficult; I'm not going to say it isn't. Think, for example, of all that I went through before I jumped off that cliff! Now think of the cliffs that you face in your life, which are keeping you from achieving your goals. Then ask yourself again—what "cliffs" do you need to jump off to move forward in life and become the type of person that you want to be?

With a much more severe consequence then cliff jumping, Martin Luther King put his fears aside and did what was right despite what he knew could ultimately happen. He lost his life in the process, but ultimately freed millions of people from oppression.

Neil Armstrong and the other astronauts aboard Apollo 11 had no guarantees that they would safely return home to earth when they boarded the rocket aimed at the moon. Heroes such as Martin Luther King and Neil Armstrong prove to us that regardless of what our fears are, we can overcome them and achieve great things.

Eliminating or even greatly reducing fear must take place for you to continue to move forward in the pursuit of your goals and your destiny. Review my *Fear Destruction Process* whenever you feel "frozen" with fear.

Finally, I can think of no better message of plowing forward in life, in pursuit of your goals despite your level of fear, than what Frank Herbert said:

"I must not fear.
Fear is the mind-killer.
Fear is the little-death that
brings total obliteration.
I will face my fear.
I will permit it to pass over me
and through me.
And when it has gone past I will
turn the inner eye to see its path.
Where the fear has gone
there will be nothing.
Only I will remain."

What I believe that he means is that, when we face our fears, we learn to somehow overcome them. As a result, we are no longer fearful. In the process of going through these struggles we become more confident in every area of our life.

My belief is that your heart knows what is best for you, so you need to listen to this calling and move forward pursuing whatever it is that your heart is calling you to—despite your fears. It is okay to be afraid, just as long as you make certain that your fear does not stop you! I challenge you to listen to your heart, put your fears aside, and go!

CHAPTER 8

Remembering Those Who Molded You

"Who, being loved, is poor?"
— Oscar Wilde

Now that you have a positive and grateful understanding of the people and things that you're blessed with in life, and know that the "down" times are only temporary, you're free to pursue your destiny—a destiny that will be very different from anyone else's!

But wait! Please remember this important point: As you pursue your goals, PLEASE don't forget who the truly important people are in your life, your family and your close friends. We often get too caught up in pursuing our dreams and reaching our destiny that we sometimes forget these important people. While you pursue your goals, you must stop and remember that to be loved, one must love. After all, love is a verb!

I was sent the following poem via e-mail from a friend. It has left quite an impression on me (even though it came from the Internet and was written by an unknown author):

Around the corner I have a friend
In this great city that has no end.
Yet the days go by and the weeks rush on,
And before I know it a year is gone!

And I never see my old friend's face,
For life is a swift and terrible race.
He knows I like him just as well,
As in the days when I rang his bell.

And he rang mine, though we were younger then,
And now we are busy tired men.
Tired of playing a foolish game,
Tired of trying to make a name.

"Tomorrow," I say, "I will call Jim,"
Just to show that I'm thinking of him.
But tomorrow comes and tomorrow goes,
And the distance between us grows and grows.

Around the corner—yet miles away,
Here's a telegram, sir: "Jim died today."
And that is what we get and deserve in the end,
Around the corner, a vanished friend!

Therefore, remember to always say what you mean. If you love someone, tell them. Don't be afraid to express yourself. Reach out and tell that someone what they mean to you. Because when you decide that it is the right time, it may be too late! Seize the day, never have regrets. Most importantly, stay close to your friends and family, for they have helped make you the person you are today!

This is a very touching poem—after all, your friends and family are the ones who can bring you more *love* in your life, if you stay close to them over the years. Everyone yearns for more *love* in their life so always try and keep in touch with your loved ones.

EXERCISE

Who are the people—family, friends, and acquaintances—that have made a difference in your life?

_____

_____

_____

_____

_____

_____

_____

What steps can you take to reach out to each of these people on a regular basis?

_____

_____

_____

_____

_____

_____

Are there any people / friends in your life who are in need in some way? If so, what can you do to help?

_____

_____

_____

_____

_____

_____

_____

FRIENDS MAKE A DIFFERENCE

My best friend is a guy named Dave Beauchamp. We've known each other since the third grade; in fact, my mother and his father went to high school together in the 1950s in Flint, Michigan. Back when our family's house burned, it was Dave and his mother, Kathy, who organized a school food drive for our family (Kathy was an extremely caring and loving person—like a second mother to me until she passed away in May 1985). We had just moved out of a hotel and into a rental home for the summer, and I can remember my mother's tears of joy as Dave and his mother delivered at least 30 bags of groceries to our temporary home while our house was being repaired.

After college, I helped Dave by forwarding his resume to someone I knew. That person later hired him!

Dave and I continue to be close today. In fact, a month never goes by without one of us calling each other. In 1996,

Dave came to Seattle on a business trip. At the time I was deliberating as to whether to begin doing public speaking again and even pondering writing a book. Dave encouraged me. "You have a good story to tell," he said, "and people will listen!"

I have always cherished his words and have used them as an inspiration along my journey. Thank you, Dave! The friendships we nourish help us to get more *happiness* in our lives. Our friendship reminds me of what Abraham Lincoln said in 1849:

**"The better part of one's life,
consists of his friendships."**

Dave's words inspired me to write this book. If you too have a good story to tell and desire to become a published author, please visit my Web site **www.CreateYourOwnDestiny.com** and click on "Publishing Help" to see how I can help you become published. Through Dave and my speaking coach, Albert Mensah, I learned that people just want to be entertained in life through stories (movies, books, video games, etc).

Therefore, I encourage you to never forget all of those great times and stories that you have shared with your family and friends over the years. Ultimately, someday all that we will have left is our stories. This is one reason why I love speaking to older folks so much—to listen and learn from their stories and wisdom!

Like Dave and Albert have done for me, I would like you to think of others in your life in addition to your close friends who may have encouraged you as well. Maybe a *coach* or a *teacher* perhaps, or possibly a *minister*.

Two men that I would like to acknowledge for their efforts in molding me are Bill McCarrick and Rob Van Pelt. Bill coached me in football and baseball throughout elementary and junior high school. Rob coached me in football and basketball in high school. Both of these individuals worked for the local schools near my hometown, but they also coached as a way of giving something back to their community. These two taught me what competition and team work are all about. They also taught me that winning isn't everything, but what's most important is simply putting forth your best effort in an attempt to win. This is really the definition of success. Both always inspired me to go the extra mile and not fall into the trap of mediocrity! Both have wonderful families of their own, but yet, they always treated me like one of their sons.

Because of the principles that these two wonderful men instilled in me at a very young age, I was able to take this knowledge and confidence with me into the business world. When I had my back injury early in college (which ended my football career), because of what these two coaches taught me:

I was able to transfer my athletic discipline into my academics and later my career.

Because of this knowledge, I feel that I have a tremendous advantage over my competition in the business world. Thank you Bill! Thank you Rob! They are two great men! In fact, it was Rob Van Pelt who best taught me the difference between winning and losing with this statement:

"The difference between winners and losers is that winners show up *expecting* to win, while losers show up *hoping* to win!"

Because of them, today I help coach my kids' youth basketball and baseball teams. I try to instill in these children the same messages that they once taught me.

I can only hope that, as my children grow older, and begin school sports, they will get to someday play for someone like Bill and Rob.

EXERCISE

Think of a friend who's helped you with words and support. What can you do to say "thank you" to this friend?

_____

_____

_____

_____

_____

Now think of other close friends of yours: What can you do to help inspire and support them?

_____

_____

_____

_____

_____

FAMILY MAKES A DIFFERENCE

All of us have that someone special in our life, be it a mother or a grandparent. The question then must be what is it that you are doing (or what can you do) to show that person that you are grateful for what they have done for you over the years to make you the person that you are today? My parents have both recently retired and, like many retired couples in good health, they are somewhat concerned about their long-term financial situation. I can't even imagine how much money they have spent on me from birth through college, but I have a deep desire to help them out in return any way I can. I would love to win the lottery and then give them half the winnings. They have told me that they do not need my help, but I still have a desire to do so in one way or another. However, you don't need to compensate or "repay" those who molded you. Instead, how about writing nice two-page letters from your heart thanking the people for all that they have done for you. You'll be surprised how appreciative this message will be in their eyes.

Lastly, visit your family as often as possible or help them visit you. Accept them for who they are, and whatever you do, *don't* try to change them! Love them for who they are and always be grateful for what they have done for you!

I have also learned how powerful and comforting it can be to speak with my parents often over the phone and continually seek out their advice.

SUMMARY

Remembering those who helped mold you is an important part of being able to "give something back" in life. What's more, you can use your positive experiences from people who have helped you in your efforts to help others. The world will truly be a much better place if we think of ourselves less, and instead think about—and assist—others as much as possible. It was Zig Ziglar who said:

"The key to getting everything in life that you want, is simply to help enough other people get what they want."

Zig's quote is so true. People only care how much you know when they know how much you care. Therefore NEVER forget those who have helped mold you along the way. If you can't find a way to make it up to them, please mentor a young person and show them the way, just as someone once did for you. This person will be eternally grateful for your time and energy. One of the best investments we can all make is to spend time with the youth of today, because they will become the leaders of tomorrow!

Remember, we are incapable of changing another human being regardless of how much we may want to in many cases. **If you want to influence another person or an organization, then you must "be" the change that you wish to see. This is the true meaning of leadership!**

Finally, I encourage you to get a photo of each person that has positively impacted your life, and then frame these pictures and place them on your wall in your home office. This will become your "Wall of Fame" and serve as a reminder to remember those who molded you.

CHAPTER 9

Executing Your Plan Daily

"Find something that you love to do, and you will never have to work another day the rest of your life!"

— Harvey MacKay

Up to this point we have done a lot of dreaming, planning, goal-setting, and laying the financial and motivational groundwork for our destiny. But planning is never enough—at some point a person must act.

Not all actions must be physical actions. They can be mental as well. Mental actions are called *decisions*, and are as equally important in creating your own destiny as physical actions.

My father always used to tell me that when faced with a situation or opportunity, even by not making a decision to take one action or another is actually a decision—in this case, to not do anything about the situation.

You have heard (I'm sure) the old saying:

"Those who hesitate in life, lose!"

It's similar to being in a car waiting to pull out into traffic. If you spot an opening, you either stay or go. If you drive out halfway into traffic, and *then* decide to pull back or if you hesitate, you're more likely to be hit by another car. The same is true in life.

This reminds me of how I received a very lucrative job (primarily because of the stock options). At the time, I wasn't really looking for a job, as I was very happily employed by Toppan Electronics. But, a recruiter had been calling me over the previous several weeks trying to get me excited about a sales position with Merix. Well, one day about 10:30 a.m., I received a call from John Cavanaugh, a sales manager at Merix. He was in town and had a lunch appointment just cancel, so he called to ask if I would be interested in meeting with him for lunch as an informal first interview. At first I declined, thinking, *Why should I spend an hour in the car (each way) to meet someone from another organization when I am very content with my current position?* I hung up the phone, but then thought to myself: *He who hesitates in life, loses!* I immediately called him back to confirm our lunch appointment.

To make a long story short, this first lunch appointment laid the foundation for eventually getting a job offer. This was the first company that I made over six figures in annual salary and commissions, and it was the first one to give me a significant amount of stock options as well (all because I didn't hesitate). Instead, I took immediate action (I had only hung up the phone for about two seconds before calling him back) and went after the opportunity which had been presented to me. Your opportunity may also appear this quickly, so it is important not to hesitate, instead execute immediately!

Opportunities are never lost. They are just found by other people who take quick action!

You can also think of taking action another way: You've copied songs from various artists onto a tape or CD. The songs are all there, ready to be heard. But it's only when you press the "Play" button that you can hear the music and the fruits of your hard work. That's what taking action is: hitting the "Play" button in your life.

I know what many of you are probably thinking right now: *I'm too busy*, or *That's easy for you to say, but I have two jobs, a spouse, kids and other responsibilities which take up my time.* Or, *I take evening classes, so I don't have the time.*

All of us have time constraints. The key is to accept this fact and still move forward, even if only a little bit each and every day. Here's an old saying that might help you: *Life is hard, but inch by inch, life is a cinch!* Henry Ford once said:

"Nothing is particularly hard if you divide it into small jobs."

It doesn't matter how fast you are moving toward your goals. The real key is that you are moving toward your goals steadily, on a daily basis, because over time this daily involvement can and will add up and produce results. Each daily action, no matter how small, will bring you one step closer to your destiny.

Still think you can't do something every day? Here are a few of the many simple things you can do each day to move yourself closer to your destiny:

- Review your goals.
- Make a phone call or send an e-mail.

- Read a section from a motivational book or a book related to your destiny.

- Schedule one 15-minute session alone to brainstorm new ideas.

- Write for 20 minutes on something related to your destiny, such as updating your resume, working on a business plan, or simply writing a letter to a potential client or partner.

- Edit and review something you have previously written.

- Research needed information on the Internet or at the library.

- Discuss your ideas with other like-minded people and build a team.

There are many, many ways to take action each and every day. This is critical to success, because ACTION EQUALS RESULTS. One of my favorite quotes regarding action comes from an unknown source:

"If you knew what you did today, could change the way you feel tomorrow, would you act differently?"

That's right—I guarantee that if you take some small actions every day toward your destiny, these small acts, when added up over five or 10 years, will produce valuable results. In fact, I believe you'll not simply meet your goals, you'll far exceed them!

Think about it this way—there is no such thing as overnight success. In fact, Susan Friedmann (an author friend of mine) has said that:

"Overnight success takes 10-15 years!"

I believe that this is true if you do one action item per day in pursuit of your passion and destiny. Imagine however, if you broke a sweat and you did just two things per day in pursuit of your goals, you could achieve success in five to seven years. If you did three action items per day, it may take only three to five years.

For example, this book that you are reading is the result of nothing more than me writing a little bit here, a little bit there, in the early morning or late into the evening—over a five-year time frame! I began in 1996 and finished this in 2001. There were many times that several months would pass in which I didn't write at all because I got caught up in doing too many other things (including a vigorous travel schedule with my day job). But as you can see, the results of executing little by little over time can result in something significant! This book has now sold over 60,000 copies and has helped thousands of people all over the world pursue their passions and create their own destiny. It happened for me, and I am confident that your daily actions of executing your game plan can produce equally great results.

EXERCISE

Think of your goals and destiny, then list five ways you can execute your plan on any given day:

1.

2.

3.

4.

5.

TAKING RISKS

One potential drawback to taking action is the necessity, in many cases, of taking one or more risks. Taking a risk can be scary—there is the possibility of failing, of looking inept or unprepared.

But taking risks must be done to move toward your destiny. Here's another one of my favorite quotes, by George Elliot, that I learned from Successories (my favorite motivational company; call them at (800) 535-2773 for a catalogue, or visit them on the web at: www.Successories.com) with this in mind:

"Only those who will risk going too far, can possibly find out how far they can go!"

I believe that if you are going to get what you want, then you must execute your plan and you can't *wait* for your ship to come in. I believe that when your ship comes in, it will not come all the way in to the shore. Think of all the cruise ships you see—many always stay anchored about one mile off shore when visiting small islands. Therefore, when your ship comes in, you are going to have to muster up the courage to leave the shore and swim out after it, if you want to reach your destiny.

Another Successories quote that I believe further drives this point home:

"You can not discover new oceans unless you have the courage to lose sight of the shore."

EXERCISE

Reflect for a moment about a risk you faced at one time in your life. What fears or other emotions were present as you studied this risk?

_____

_____

_____

_____

What either prevented you from moving forward or propelled you to act despite the risk?

_____

_____

_____

_____

What lessons from this instance can still help you when facing future risks?

_____

_____

_____

_____

Risks must be taken and overcome to secure your destiny. Because this is the case, THE TRUE RISK LIES IN NOT TAKING RISKS. Take educated risks. Don't worry about "failing"—that's just a word. There is no real "failure" in life—but there are lessons. Move forward embracing risks. You'll be happy with the results. You need to execute daily— despite risk!

FINDING MORE TIME

We've just discussed risk taking. Now I'd like to show you how to find more *time* in your day.

Whenever I discuss execution of a plan on a daily basis, people almost always say the same thing: "Patrick, I don't have the time." Some people would view this as a legitimate reason. I don't—I think this is an excuse.

If you truly don't have extra time in your life right now, then you _really_ need to execute your plan and pursue a destiny that will give you more time later.

If you fall into this category—where you use excuses to not do something—here are some ways to find more *time* on a daily basis to execute your game plan:

- Turn off the television. If you do watch TV, only watch those programs related to your goals. For example, watch the Biography channel to learn how people you admire have overcome tremendous odds and overwhelming adversities to achieve great things in their lives.

- Carry whatever book you are reading with you at all times. Then, when you find yourself with unexpected free time, such as waiting for someone to show up for an appointment, you won't waste that time—you can use it to read about your destiny-related topic.

- Carry a cell phone with you at all times. Again, this gives you the ability to make and receive calls during "down" or "transition" times, or at other moments where you normally might have wasted time.

- Limit small talk. It's fun to chat with friends and family. But too much small talk can steal precious moments from your day. Don't be impolite, but limit small talk as much as possible, especially at work—a good way to do this is to close your office door.

- Don't sleep-in on weekends. A great time I've found to work on my dreams is on Saturday and Sunday mornings between 6 a.m. and 9 a.m., before my kids are up and ready to go. The satisfaction of starting your day working toward your dreams is hard to describe!

- Limit Internet surfing. Don't surf unless you're looking for something specific to your goals or destiny. Your time is valuable; don't waste it online.

- Keep your computer free of viruses, annoying pop-up ads, and Internet hijackers. You can lose all kinds of time and productivity if you are continuously dealing with these problems.

- Give up sports news. Sports scores and statistics can be addicting (I know). Which would you rather be: someone who knows all the batting averages of the top 20 players in Major League Baseball, with no money in the bank, or a millionaire who doesn't know which team is most likely to win the Stanley Cup?

- Take control of your lunch hours. This can be some excellent time to work on your dream. Try to schedule a lunch meeting as often as possible with people you know who are capable of helping you accomplish your dreams.

- Hire a housekeeper. This is an expense, of course. But the question to consider is this: where is your time more valuably spent—cleaning your bathroom, or working on your dream?

All of these ideas will surely help you find more time in your day / week. Use this "found" time to execute your game plan. As stated earlier, it's important to realize that if you don't have any time now, you HAD BETTER make certain that the successful implementation of your plan will give you more time later. Otherwise, 20 years will pass and you will be in the same situation that you are now.

This reminds me of the rat race story. If you ever watch a gerbil on a running wheel, you know what I'm talking about. A gerbil can get on that wheel and run like mad for 20 seconds (or even 20 minutes), only to get off and realize that it's in the exact same spot as when he began. Well, what is the difference between you and a gerbil? You could run on the corporate wheel (rat race) for 20 years and make little, if any, real "progress"—i.e., be in basically the same spot as when you started, although now you'll be 20 years older. Or, would you rather make time to pursue a destiny that will give you more *time*, more *money*, and more *freedom*?

To better understand this rat race phenomenon, I recommend that you read two books by Robert Kiyosaki: *Rich Dad, Poor Dad* and *The Cashflow Quadrant*. Then play his game called *Cashflow 101*, which teaches you that the only way to win in life is to get out of the "rat race" sooner rather than later.

EXECUTE TODAY AND BENEFIT TOMORROW

There's an old saying that goes:

**"If you do what you have always done, then
you will get what you have always gotten!"**

If you are to truly become free, then you must execute your plan daily; otherwise, you will one day die an unfulfilled person! That's not what I want for you—I want you to achieve all of your goals and destiny!

Another thought: here's a (humorous-but-true) definition of insanity I once heard somewhere:

**"Doing the same thing over and over,
and expecting different results!"**

If you are to truly experience your destiny, then you must—without question—put your excuses and pains aside and execute your plan daily! As Bill McCarrick, the best football coach I ever had, used to say:

**"You have to play when you're hurt,
if you want to win!"**

Sooner or later, you will learn that ALL of those who have achieved tremendous feats in life have, at one time or another, "played hurt."

Pursuing your destiny and executing your plan daily is bound to "hurt" at times, but the rewards in terms of goals achieved and destinies created will be more than worth it!

DAILY EXECUTION

An example of my daily execution that I am sure I will never forget occurred in November of 1994 when I had the opportunity to meet THE PRESIDENT OF THE UNITED STATES—Bill Clinton. Believe it or not, I was the one who made this happen. I knew that if I could put myself in the right spot, at the right time, a brief encounter would be inevitable. In other words, I turned this opportunity into a reality.

This is what happened. My family and I attended a very large church when we lived in Seattle. In the weeks previous to the encounter, I learned that the President would be visiting the church during his campaign for re-election. Therefore, I marked my calendar book to make certain that I didn't miss service that weekend.

When I awoke that morning, I told my wife that I was going to meet the President today! I made it a point to show up almost 30 minutes early to ensure getting a center-aisle seat, as I figured that he might walk down the center aisle at the conclusion of the service.

To make a long story short, the President made a side entrance surrounded by at least a dozen Secret Service agents. At the conclusion of the service, the President and his bodyguards exited the church via the center aisle where I was seated. He was moving at a speed that was almost a jog. It was obvious he was NOT stopping to shake anyone's hands, nor did he have any intentions of doing so. But he had obviously not met Patrick Snow before!

Being the opportunist that I am, I wasn't going to be content just letting him walk by without a handshake! Therefore, I stepped out into the aisle, leading with my right arm open—ready for a handshake. As I did this, I could see all the Secret Service agents flinch! Once they determined that I was harmless, they backed off. I extended my arm to shake hands with the President and said "My name is Patrick Snow, it is nice to meet you!" He embraced my right hand with a firm handshake and then placed his left hand on my right forearm, and said "It is nice to meet you, Patrick!"

Just as this occurred (unbeknownst to me), the church photographer stepped out into the aisle behind us, and took a picture of our handshake as we looked each other in the eye. The President then quickly rushed out the back of the church and jumped in his limousine (not shaking another hand along the way). To my surprise, this photo was placed on the front page of the church newspaper. I eventually was given the original photo as a keepsake (it also helps prove to my friends that this brief encounter really occurred). The point of this example is that because of my advanced planning, preparation, and execution of my plan, I was able to make this event unfold and become a reality!

I simply saw the invisible (the future as I desired it to be), and consequently (because my actions were now almost second nature to me) I was able to accomplish the impossible! Whether you know it or not, you, too, have this same ability. All you have to do to put this into action is believe in yourself and execute daily!

It was a great sermon, by the way, but I was there only to meet the President of the United States!

How many people can say that not only were they photographed with a President of the United States, but they also had their photo with the President on the front page of a newspaper? Can you imagine if I had decided to sleep in on that Sunday morning, instead of meeting the President? What could you accomplish if you woke up early every weekend morning? I have written (and rewritten) this book almost entirely during the weekday and weekend mornings before my children awake.

I challenge you to execute each day as if you had only 30 days to live! You will be amazed by how much you can accomplish in such a short amount of time if you incorporate this sense of urgency. You will ultimately create your own destiny faster than you could have ever imagined!

SUMMARY

The daily execution of your game plan on a consistent basis is the MOST important key to successfully creating your own destiny in life! Therefore, you must then ask yourself, if you are not executing your plan daily, what goals you are not hitting, and what opportunities you are missing simply because of a lack of daily execution. Then ask yourself what is holding you back. Once you learn what your obstacles are, then do everything in your power to overcome them. If you find that it is a lack of knowledge or experience that is holding you back, then either learn how to do the task at hand or hire someone more talented than you to get the job done right!

If you execute your plan daily over the course of five to 10 years, then I guarantee that you will not only meet all of your goals, but you will also far surpass them. This kind of achievement is what I call "under-promising and over-delivering"!

I will conclude this chapter with one of my favorite quotes from Mark Twain, which shows the importance of taking risks as you execute your plans in pursuit of your destiny:

RISK

Twenty years from now
you will be more disappointed
by the things you didn't do
than by the ones you did do.
So throw off your bowlines.
Sail away from the safe harbour.
Catch the trade winds in your sails.
Explore. Dream. Discover.

CHAPTER 10

Launching Your New Business

**"Act boldly and unseen forces
will come to your aid."**

— Brian Tracy

Now what? Well, hopefully as a result of reading this book you have come to the same conclusion I have: that it's virtually impossible to create your own destiny as an employee at a job. However, as a business owner, I believe your chances of getting more *time*, more *money*, more *freedom*, more *health*, more *love*, and more *happiness* in life increase dramatically.

As I pointed out in chapter four, my solution for attaining wealth today is to own and operate your own business. Owning your own business is not just a good idea, it is a necessity if you desire to get ahead and create long term financial peace of mind as you plan for retirement. I sincerely believe what business consultant Brent Brodine says about this topic:

**"Retiring with a million dollars is not a luxury,
but a necessity!"**

If you are reading this book and are a thriving business owner, feel free to skip this chapter and move on to the next.

If you are already a small business owner but are *not* achieving the success you desire, then I'm confident you will receive great ideas and insights within this chapter.

If, however, you are unhappy at work and are looking to start your own business, or at least want to explore business ownership, then this chapter might be the most important chapter of this book for you. (If you have made it this far into the book and still don't know what kind of business to launch, I recommend that you visit my website, **www.CreateYourOwnDestiny.com** and click on "Free Stuff," then click "50 Home-Based Business Ideas" to further help you sort through the many businesses opportunities you can pursue.)

I hope you took the previous chapter to heart when I wrote that success may take longer than overnight. Well, launching a successful business is no different! I do believe, however, that anyone can be successful in launching a business if that business is one in which they are passionate about and believe in. Successful businesses take time, money, energy, and most of all *action*, and *action springs from passion!*

In this chapter, I will outline how to do all of the above without spending a bunch of money. Use this chapter as a blueprint to give you the BEST chance of being successful in your new business. I also recommend that you leverage the Internet and use it as a strategic resource to increase your business's chance of success. This chapter is designed to offer many strategies on how to successfully launch a new business, while using the Internet as your business partner.

SEVEN DESIRABLE TRAITS FOR BUSINESS OWNERSHIP

In the process of appearing as a featured radio guest on hundreds of radio stations across North America (addressing unhappy workers), I am constantly asked what I believe to be the BEST business someone can get involved with. I believe there is no one "right" business that you can start, but I do believe the best kinds of businesses share these "seven desirable traits," in which you can:

- Run from the comfort of your home (on your schedule)

- Match to your passions (you can't be successful doing something you don't enjoy)

- Operate without having to hire employees (you don't want to be a baby-sitter)

- Get started for a low investment (franchises can cost hundreds of thousands of dollars)

- Make money whether you are working or sleeping (a Web store provides flexibility)

- Build without having to purchase huge amounts of inventory (garages are for cars)

- Utilize the **INTERNET** (as your store front to sell your products and services 24 hours per day, seven days per week, on a global basis)

I believe there are a million ways to make a million dollars. All it takes is for you to properly execute one way. While there are thousands of great businesses out there, many of which share the traits just mentioned, to me three areas stand out: Real Estate Investing (because of real estate appreciation), Network Marketing (due to teamwork and residual income), and perhaps my favorite, operating an Internet Marketing Business (with the resulting ability to reach the global marketplace 24/7).

ROAD MAP TO START A SUCCESSFUL BUSINESS

In Doug Hall's book, *Jump Start Your Business Brain*, Doug mentions that too many people get involved in business without adequately doing their due diligence. This due diligence gives them the best chances for success. In fact, he says that many get involved in businesses when the odds are stacked against them. He says that you have a better chance of winning in a casino than succeeding in some business models. If you are going to gamble, he says that Roulette is your best odds at 47 percent.

I believe that if you follow these 20 suggestions (which I have developed over the years as a result of both my business successes and setbacks), your chances of success are far better than 47 percent. If you skip over these, you might as well just go to a casino where you may have better odds.

1. Pursue Most Marketable Passions
2. Get Emotional Support from Spouse (or Family)
3. Perform a Feasibility Study
4. Know Your Target Market
5. Take Advantage of All Tax Deductions
6. Minimize Business Expenses
7. Focus on Marketing
8. Don't Waste Money on Advertising
9. Budget Three Times the Money and Time
10. You May Have to Risk More Than You Think
11. Align Yourself with People More Talented Than You
12. Grow Your Business Through Relationships and Referrals
13. Create a Publicity Buzz
14. Determine Your Exit Strategy
15. Get a Coach or Mentor
16. Join or Create a Master Mind Group

17. Determine Your Solution
18. Leverage the Internet
19. Get Started on Execution
20. Never Give Up Until You Win

<u>Pursue Most Marketable Passions</u>: I believe it's virtually impossible to become successful building something in which you lack belief. If you are passionate about something, chances are you'll stick with it through good times and bad. The best way to do this is to turn your hobbies into your business. Inventory your hobbies and ask yourself which could make money if you position your hobby as a business. Next, take the necessary steps to transition your hobby into your business.

<u>Get Emotional Support from Spouse (or Family)</u>: It is vitally important to receive support from your spouse or significant other early on in your business, because you will have to work long hours and at the beginning you may also have to spend more money than you make. With your spouse's blessing, you can work together towards achieving your vision. However, getting that blessing may be harder than you think, as there are a lot of cynics out there who do not believe it is possible to succeed in business. I recommend that you show your spouse examples of other ordinary people who have succeeded in business. In doing this, your spouse may come to realize that eventually they may get to work out of choice, as opposed working out of need—as a result of your businesses success.

<u>Perform a Feasibility Study</u>: This is what you do prior to launching your business to ensure your success before getting started. This includes writing a business plan and creating a marketing plan (which are two different things). In your feasibility study, you will uncover the true costs of launching

your business. Knowing this information from the beginning will increase your chances of success. This is one of the most important steps and should not be skipped.

Know Your Target Market: It is extremely important to properly identify who exactly is going to purchase your product or service so that you can uncover their needs and use your solution to improve their life in one way or another. If you miss this step, you are almost certainly setting yourself up for failure. The best way to conduct market research to is to simply interview potential buyers—just ask people what it is that they want, and find out if they can currently get it. If they can't, perhaps your business can ease their pain.

Take Advantage of All Tax Deductions: The free enterprise system in the United States is ideally suited for business owners, but many simply overlook the many available tax deductions due to a lack of knowledge. For example, the following expenses are partially deductible for home-based business owners: mortgage payment, business expenses, computer expenses, mileage or vehicle usage, phone, utilities, Internet, and travel expenses.

Minimizing Business Expenses: Growing a business can be very costly! But building this business (which becomes your asset) can support you for dozens of years to come. It can become one of the best investments that you can ever make! Therefore, make capital expenditure decisions that will provide a solid return on your investment. Not all expenditures result in income. For many businesses, for example, advertising can be an unjustified expense.

Focus on Marketing: Marketing is very effective and many times doesn't cost a lot of money. Marketing your business can take many different shapes and forms. The key is to maximize your efforts and expand your reach to as many people as possible. For example, it does not cost money to post flyers or put business cards on community bulletin boards. One of the best marketing experts in the world is Dan Kennedy. I encourage you to visit his site and read his books to become a marketing expert. His site is www.DanKennedy.com.

Don't Waste Money on Advertising: Advertising costs a ton of money and many times is ineffective. When my destiny message was featured on the cover story of *USA Today* on December 5th, 2002, I learned that marketing flat out works! However, in that same issue, I am sure there were business owners who had spent thousands of dollars placing ads in the back of the paper who may not have received any calls. Stay clear from advertising sales people unless you have an unlimited budget. A perfect example to help you distinguish the difference between marketing and advertising is that you want your Web site listed with search engines (spending money doing so would be good marketing dollars spent). However, listing your Web address on another Web site as an ad would be advertising dollars spent and would be a waste of money in my opinion.

Budget Three Times the Money and Time: If you think that you are going to be able to invest $5,000 in your business and make tons of money in the first six months, you may be correct. If you plan on this allocation, ultimately your investment may end up being $15,000 and it may take 18 months to receive huge returns. The reason that this is important is that ultimately your business may take longer than you want to be successful, costing you more money as a result. However, I can assure you that this extra time and money is a good investment to attain the kind of freedom a business can provide.

You May Have to Risk More Than You Think: Nothing worthwhile in life comes without risk. Howard Schultz risked every asset he had, and every asset he didn't have, to launch Starbucks. Today his company is a multi-billion dollar company and he also owns The Seattle Supersonics. The bottom line is this: successful people take risks! If you want to become wealthy, then you too must take risks. Ask yourself this question: what are you willing risk, to get what you want?

Align Yourself with People More Talented Than You: The smartest business owners hire people even more intelligent than themselves to help grow their business. Once your team is in place, then you must delegate. Additionally, if you don't know how to do something, then contract that work out, like your tax preparation for example. A great place to meet extremely talented people is to attend or join local networking groups. You will find that these kinds of groups are filled with successful entrepreneurs. You may not hire these types as full-time employees, but you can certainly seek their assistance to help you grow your business.

Grow Your Business Through Relationships and Referrals: You must develop relationships with prospects to close sales. To do so, gain trust, respect, and qualify need, as I have outlined in my Sales Success Formula in Chapter Four. Zig Ziglar says: "If people like you they'll listen to you, but if they trust you, they'll do business with you." Bottom line is this: people buy from whom they like. When you make more friends, you make more sales. It's that simple! Encourage satisfied customers to help you attract more business. Reward your clients when they give you qualified leads. As a result, you can eventually create a complete business by referral. Brian Buffini's referral program teaches small business owners to do "client appreciation dinners" as a way of keeping leads coming in the door. Mr. Buffini's site is www.ProvidenceSeminars.com.

Create a Publicity Buzz: In S. Truett's book, *Eat Mor Chikin, Inspire More People*, the founder discusses how his company, Chick-fil-A, spent a small amount of money on billboards around the Atlanta area displaying images of cows painting the billboard which read, "Eat Mor Chikin" and "Five out of Five Cows Agree, Eat Mor Chikin." As a result, his company received literally millions of dollars worth of FREE publicity via radio, newspapers, and TV because he successfully created a buzz about his company. This is the kind of thing that gets the media's attention. Do something creative like this, then pitch your press releases to the media. If you need help with press releases, email Tim Polk at PolkPar72@aol.com.

Determine Your Exit Strategy: The goal is retirement, plain and simple! When do you want to retire and with how much money? Many people never put a time frame on this objective. Therefore, I believe it is important to understand how much money you will need to retire. More importantly, to then place a date on when you will retire and walk away. Ideally, you will want your business to create you a residual income to allow you to continue making money long after retirement.

Get a Coach or Mentor: It is easier and more economical to learn from other people's mistakes than to repeat them yourself. For this reason, I believe it is crucial to find someone you can trust who is in business for themself, and ask them to help you as you launch your business. You would be surprised how many people are willing to help if only asked. Business coaches come in all flavors. I encourage you to also visit a networking group in your area where you'll find local coaches willing to help you out. A national coaching organization worth looking into is Building Champions. Their site is www.BuildingChampions.com.

Join or Create a Master Mind Group: Napoleon Hill is the father of the master mind concept. In his book, *Law of Success*, he states that a Master Mind can be created through the bringing together, in the spirit of harmony, two or more minds. Out of this "blending of the minds" creates a third mind, which may be appropriated and used by one or all of the individual minds. This process, or third mind, will provide insights or ideas that may not come to light without such a mastermind group. I am in two master mind groups and both have been very beneficial to my growth as an entrepreneur.

Determine Your Solution: It is extremely important to know what your product or service value proposition is—in other words, what problem does your product or service solve for your clients. This is important to identify for your business to be successful. If you don't know what pain your product or service relieves in the marketplace, you may never succeed in business. Your company must solve other people's needs. In doing so, these clients will tell others about you, and your company will continue to grow.

Leverage the Internet: You can't be everywhere all of the time and for that reason it is important to leverage the Internet by having a solid Web site with a high ranking on a search engine to bring prospects to your Web store. More details on Web sites, the Internet, and search engines follow later in this chapter. However, if you are not a technical person, I highly encourage you to leverage another person or company's expertise and have them build and maintain your site instead of spending time doing this yourself. You could spend thousands of hours on your site, but this is time that you could be marketing your business instead. I encourage you to evaluate the next section on the huge increases in the number of Web sites world wide (which is currently over 60 million and growing quite rapidly).

Get Started on Execution: Getting started in business can be a scary proposition, so much so that we must develop a high level of courage to overcome our fears and move forward. This concept reminds me of one of my favorite quotes, from an unknown source: "Courage is the ability to let go of the familiar." Get a business license, set up your company's legal structure, and start saving all your receipts for your taxes. Once this is done, make sure that you accomplish something each and every day with your business. Too many people get started in business, take a few weeks off here and there, and then never get back on track.

Never Give Up, Until You Win: Too many people give up on their dreams just inches shy of their gold mine. The world is filled with people who gave up too soon and who now remain dependent on a job to support their families. Business ownership is one of the best ways to attain wealth. However, to accomplish your goals, you must stay the course the entire way and remain committed to achieve your financial goals.

THE INTERNET

The Internet continues to experience explosive growth by people of all ages, level of business experience, and computer savvy. There is a reason why today there are more than 60 million Web sites worldwide: millions of people from all corners of the earth have found a better way to sell products and services than through traditional store fronts, which can be very costly. Take a look at the statistics below summarizing the increased number of Web sites since 1990.

A SPECIAL NOTE

World Leader in Internet Research, Robert H. Zakon Reports: Hobbes Internet Timeline Copyright © 2003 Robert H. Zakon

The Number of Web Sites in the World:

1990	1	1998	2,500,000
1992	50	2000	20,000,000
1994	10,000	2002	40,000,000
1996	250,000	2004	60,000,000

http://www.zakon.org/robert/internet/timeline/
www.zakon.org

<u>It used to be common knowledge that to be successful in business it took three things: LOCATION, LOCATION, and LOCATION. Today, this may still be true for a traditional business, but perhaps now more important than location is: WEB PRESENCE on the INTERNET! With a good Web site and online merchant store, your company location can be accessible by every person world-wide with Internet access. This kind of coverage transcends LOCATION.</u>

However, to get a good location for your Web site on the Web, you will need to use search engines to insure high placement of your site. This can be very challenging if you don't know what you are doing. Therefore, I encourage you to have your webmaster help you out with search engine placement. Many webmasters are good at *building* sites but not at *placing* sites. If this is the case in your situation, I have identified a resource which can help you with search engine placement and optimization: Stores Online (www.StoresOnline.com) which helps small businesses secure high Web placements on search engines.

In the interviews that you will read at the end of this chapter, you will find that virtually all of the business owners recommended securing a high placement on a search engine in order to grow a successful Internet business.

EXERCISE

In the spaces below, list five products or services in which you are passionate about that you can market using the Internet:

1.

2.

3.

4.

5.

UNIQUE SELLING PROPOSITION

When deciding what kinds of products or services to sell on the Internet, it is important to ask yourself WHY people will buy your product or service instead of your competitor's. You need to determine what Doug Hall calls a UNIQUE SELLING PROPOSITION so that you can set yourself apart from the others.

For example, if you decide to sell calculators on the Internet, you had better come up with a darn good reason why people should buy *your* calculators, when they could just as easily go to local office supply store and pick one up the same day.

As a professional speaker and author, I try to set myself apart from the other speakers by advising the meeting planners that, when they pay my speaking fee, I also include several free copies of my book, *Creating Your Own Destiny*, along with the fact that I cover all of my transportation costs and meals. Most speakers will try to nickel-and-dime a meeting planner to death trying to get upgrades on flights, limo rides to and from the airport, as well as dining in expensive restaurants on their dime. I cover all of these expenses and as such, meeting planners have a more enjoyable experience booking me to speak instead of my competition.

EXERCISE

Think of one of your favorite companies and list three reasons why you buy from them instead of buying from their competition:

1.

2.

3.

Now write down three reasons why people will buy your product or service (these reasons become your Unique Selling Proposition):

1.

2.

3.

SUCCESSFUL INTERNET AND WEB SITE STRATEGIES

If you were to get into a traditional business, you would be very concerned as to the appearance, location, signage, and cleanliness of your establishment. Well, an Internet marketing business is no different—your Web site serves as your "store front."

Over the years, I have learned to implement many of the strategies I'm about to share. As a result, my site **www.CreateYourOwnDestiny.com** today gets more hits than I could have only imagined a few years ago. If you implement the following strategies for your Web site, you too, will increase your chances of success.

1. Decide Your First and Second Most Desired Response
2. Secure Domain Name That Is Easy to Remember
3. Get Your Site Listed with Many Search Engines
4. Provide Something for FREE
5. Simplify Your Site
6. Have 6-8 Items on Navigation Bar
7. Provide a Newsletter Sign Up
8. Never Sell Email Addresses to Anyone
9. Send Out Newsletters on a Regular Basis
10. Always Provide "Home" Option
11. Use Third Party Endorsements on Your Home Page
12. Place Your Photo and Video on Your Site
13. Have E-Commerce Set Up to Accept Visa and MC
14. List Your Web Address on Everything
15. Have a Counting Device on Your Site
16. Evaluate Which Pages Are Being Visited
17. Ask Visitors for Feedback
18. Provide a Zoom-In Capability
19. Use a Consistent Color Theme
20. Do Not Solely Rely on Search Engines for Web Traffic

Decide Your First and Second Most Desired Responses: Your goal of your Web site must be clearly communicated to your webmaster (or whoever is building your site). I have visited plenty of great sites that educate me, but don't drive me to their Web store to buy. When people want to buy from you, your site must make it easy to do so. For example, your first desired response may be to sell your products or services, so make that the goal of your site. Your second desired response may be collect names and email addresses so that you can build a database. Whatever your goals are for your site, *it is absolutely crucial that your webmaster understand exactly what these are.* It is better to have a functional Web site that accomplishes your objectives than a really cool Web site with flash animation but which doesn't sell your products or services.

Secure Domain Name That Is Easy to Remember: Domain name is just another phrase for "Web site." An easy to remember domain name is always best. This would be something that is very memorable and of course, ends with dot com. You don't want your prospects to have a difficult time remembering your site's address. Fewer words are better than more. Additionally, you may have 5-6 different domain names pointing at the same Web site. Also, make sure that you get your first and last name dot com. If someone else has your name and has a site, contact them and perhaps they will sell it to you. The reason why you want an easy name to remember is so that when you start marketing your site, prospects can see your flyer, and remember your Web site address without having to write it down. A bad domain name would be either lengthy or difficult to remember and may be dot biz, dot net, etc… Virtually everyone can remember dot com. Also, you want to stay away from slashes in your address as it is just too hard to remember.

Get Your Site Listed with Many Search Engines: Search engines are systems on the internet that list Web sites in a specific order for prospects to view sites. Examples of search engines include Yahoo, Google, MSN, and Lycos. It is important to get your site listed on these engines if you are trying to sell products and services on the Internet. This can cost a bit of money to get set up, so if you don't know what you are doing you are better off hiring someone to help you complete this task. A Web expert can create spider words and bury them into the embedded files of your home page. Therefore, when visitors place these words in a search engine box, your site could then be listed. Not only is it important to be listed, but what you really want is a high listing since most people surfing the Web only go about ten sites deep when searching on the Web.

Provide Something for FREE: Everyone wants something for free. Many people who surf on the Web are just entertaining themselves and have no desire to buy anything. Therefore, you want these folks to refer your site to others. The best way that I have found to do this is to offer many freebies on my site. I give away at least a dozen free reports and different kinds of goal sheets. As a result, I frequently get emails from others telling me how much they appreciated my free stuff and that they have told others about my site. Ideally, the free stuff that you give away should be something that they can download. You don't want to even think about getting in the business of shipping free stuff.

Simplify Your Site: The problem with many sites today is that visitors to the site can get overwhelmed with information. In fact, they can spend so much time navigating a Web site that they never get to the Web store to purchase anything. Simple is always better than complex. Also, a simple Web site doesn't cost nearly as much as complex sites cost to build. In other words "dumb it down." Make sure that someone with a 12-year-old reading level can adequately navigate your site.

Have 6-8 Items on Navigation Bar: A navigation bar is another way of identifying your Web site's table of contents. This ties closely to the previous point: You don't want 20 things that your visitors can look at on your site, because they may leave without having gotten to your Web store. Therefore, I believe 6-8 items on your main page is ideal. I have the following items on my CreateYourOwnDestiny.com site: Home (landing page), Free Stuff, Calendar, Web Store, Speaker Kit, Media Gallery, Testimonials, and Contact Patrick.

Provide a Newsletter Sign Up: On every page of your site you should provide an option for your visitors to sign up for your newsletter. Then, to take this a step further, on your Free Stuff page you should not allow your visitors to gain access to your Free Stuff until they have inserted their email address in the section which signs them up for your newsletter. I have done this for years and have grown my database from almost nothing to several thousand using this technique. In doing so, you may wonder how many people unsubscribe from my newsletter. My experience is that every time I send out a newsletter less than one tenth of one percent unsubscribe. Creating a database of your prospects and customers is one of your most important goals as a business owner.

Never Sell Email Addresses to Anyone: Not only mention this as a disclaimer, but also make sure that you NEVER sell or give your email databases to anyone. You are trying to establish credibility and build trust with your clients so keeping their email address confidential is the best way to do so. Without having this disclaimer in small print, you will have many visitors that may want to sign up, but are reluctant due to their concerns of getting spam from other sources.

Send Out Newsletters on a Regular Basis: This is a very good way to communicate with your prospects and customers. However, make sure your newsletter has something of value to readers. You can't send out the same newsletter each time just reminding them to buy from you. If you do provide newsworthy or interesting data, then you can always pitch your message at the bottom of your newsletter. For example, I always provide five thought-provoking quotes at the very beginning of my newsletter. In doing so, I have had many respond to advise me how much they enjoyed the quotes. Additionally, it is important to include an easy to find "Unsubscribe" option in each newsletter so that if someone no longer want your newsletter they can easily remove their name. Finally, you want to make sure that your company stays in front of your prospects, but don't hammer them too often with a newsletter. Some believe that daily or weekly newsletters are good. However, I believe that every-other-week or monthly may be better so as not to annoy your subscribers.

Always Provide a "Home" Option: The "home" option takes visitors to your home page which is also called a "landing page." This is typically the first page a person sees when visiting your site. No matter where your visitor is on your site, it is important that they always be provided with the "Home" option, so that they can easily get back to the home page. Nothing is more frustrating than having to click the "back arrow" several times to get back to the landing page. Your site needs to be simple to navigate, and a "Home" option, is key to this simplicity.

Use Third Party Endorsements on Your Home Page: In my experience, I have learned that often prospects don't believe business owners, since they think that the business owner will just say whatever it takes to make a sale. Therefore, this is why third party testimonials are so important to grow your business. Prospects will believe your customers before they will believe you. I believe that you need to incorporate these third party testimonials front and center on your home page as this is more powerful than any other copy you may have on your site. In doing so, I guarantee that you will see a lift in your response. The best way to gather testimonials is to simply ask for them. Anytime you run across a customer who has enjoyed your product or service, simply ask them if you can have them send you a brief email summarizing their positive service with your company, then ask them if you can display this on your site. You will find that almost all will allow you to do so.

Place Your Photo and Video on Your Site: People like seeing who they are doing business with. However, in Internet marketing most all transactions take place between buyer and seller without the two ever meeting. I believe your photo will help your customers gain trust in you quicker than a site with no photograph. It is worth spending a hundred dollars or so to have a professional photo taken of you for your site. I also encourage you to place your photo on your business cards as well. Also, your video will more easily introduce yourself to your prospects.

Have E-Commerce Set Up to Accept Visa and MC: With over 60 million Web sites online, literally billions of dollars are spent in online purchases via credit cards. Therefore, if you are in Internet marketing, you need to make it easy for people to buy from you. The best way to make your transaction go smoothly is to get an e-commerce merchant account which will allow you to accept your clients Visa and MasterCard. I recommend that you contact ViaKlix at (800) 377-3962 or online at www.ViaKlix.com to get set up. I have used ViaKlix for a number of years and all my Web sales revenue is directly deposited into my business checking account. If you sell on eBay, you may not need to get your own e-commerce account, but I would then recommend that you get set up through Pay Pal at www.PayPal.com.

List Your Web Address on Everything: One of the greatest challenges as an Internet Marketing Business is attracting prospects to your Web site. Therefore, I recommend that you include your Web address on all of your company materials: business cards, letterhead, return address labels, license plate frames, etc. I even have a large sign of www.CreateYourOwnDestiny.com up in the back window of my car that I can put up and take down as needed. When I am traveling for business, I display my sign and everyone I pass on the freeway (or passes me) can become aware of my site. Additionally, when I park my car in parking lots, I prominently display my sign. Remember, people passing by will only have a few moments to glance at it, so this is another reason why your domain name needs to be short enough to remember with one glance. I have sold many books as a result of my sign and even landed a few speaking engagements as well.

Have a Counting Device on Your Site: A counting device simply tells you how many "hits" or visits you are receiving to your site. If you have a small counter placed at the bottom of your site, you will be able to monitor the number of visitors. The reason this is important is so you can evaluate which marketing efforts you are doing bring traffic to your site, and which strategies are not working.

Evaluate Which Pages Are Being Visited: Your webmaster can create reports for you showing which of your Web pages are being visited most. This too, is important, because you can determine then how many visitors are actually going to your Web store. Once you evaluate these reports, you can then determine if you need to make changes to your site.

Ask Visitors for Feedback: I think feedback from your Web site visitors is extremely important as it gives you a gauge on how you are doing. The best way to do this, once you have your "Free Stuff" and "Newsletter Sign Up" in place on your site, is to have your webmaster set it up so that when people sign up, you are sent an email alerting you of each new subscriber. Next, reply to this individual via email to thank them for visiting your site, ask them if you can be of additional services, ask them for feedback on your site, and most importantly, ask how they stumbled across your site in the first place (this may be the best marketing research you can do). When people purchase from your site, make sure you follow up within a week's time to ensure their satisfaction and also ask them for referrals.

Provide a Zoom-In Capability: Whatever it is that you are selling on your site, it is very important that the buyer be able to easily view your products. To do so, I recommend that you have your site built in a way that every item in which you are selling can be zoomed in on. What I mean it that when they click on the item, a much larger image of the product becomes visible on their screen. People like to see exactly what it is they are buying.

Use a Consistent Color Theme: This may be very obvious but I have seen far too many businesses where the Web site colors, business cards, and company letterhead do not match. It is important to blend all together so that you can have a consistent look throughout your business. Also, find or develop a company logo that fits your color scheme.

Do Not Solely Rely on Search Engines for Web Traffic: This may be the most important item which I have saved for last. Many people think that if they get their site listed with a search engine and have a high placement, then they will receive tons of Web traffic to their site. This is true, but high placement on search engines is a moving target. Even though you may have a high placement today, this will change on a regular basis. Therefore, it is important to have a solid search engine placement strategy, but no matter what you do, it is crucial that this be only part of your marketing efforts and not all of your efforts.

All of these Web strategies are very important and should not be overlooked. You can make it easy on yourself by instructing your webmaster to follow the above steps to insure your site's success. However, if you still need help with this, Stores Online is a solid resource (www.StoresOnline.com) that can also help you build and maintain your Web site. They will certainly follow the above steps to ensure your success and provide you with a complete Internet education.

REAL-LIFE EXAMPLES OF ENTREPRENEURS USING THE INTERNET

On the next two pages are seven ordinary people with limited or no advanced education or training on the Internet making money from home using the Internet to market their products and services:

Name & Web site:	Tim from California (www.ProfitPress.com)
Kind of Business:	Selling e-books from Web store to contractors
Office Location:	From home
Before Launching Business:	Freelance writer and editor
Months to Profitability:	Four
Unique Selling Proposition:	Contractor-friendly information in a concise format
Challenges:	Getting large amounts of traffic to Web store
Internet Benefits:	Selling electronic files so there is NO inventory
Hours Worked:	Part-time
Advice to Others:	Partner with someone who knows the Web very well
Monthly Income:	$500 per month (biggest month $2,000)

Name & Web site:	Mary from Massachusetts (www.ToleSampler.com)
Kind of Business:	Selling art and custom-painted items on web
Office Location:	From home
Before Launching Business:	Chemistry Teacher
Months to Profitability:	12
Unique Selling Proposition:	Customized hand painted, original artwork
Challenges:	Getting more traffic to Web site
Internet Benefits:	Ability to market art to a world-wide market
Hours Worked:	Full time
Advice to Others:	Must sell something that you are passionate about
Monthly Income:	$1,000 per month (biggest month was $2,500)

Name & Web site:	Mike from Montana (www.ebay.com)
Kind of Business:	Selling clothes, CD's, electronics, and artifacts on ebay
Office Location:	From home
Before Launching Business:	Mortgage Broker
Months to Profitability:	Two
Unique Selling Proposition:	Has developed a strong track record on ebay for delivering
Challenges:	Finding valuable items for cheap to sell at large profits
Internet Benefits:	Ability to reach buyers all over the world
Hours Worked:	Part-time in between other projects
Advice to Others:	Shop at department close out sales to maximize profits
Monthly Income:	$850 per month (biggest month was $2,500)

Name & Web site:	Thomas from Washington (www.ebay.com)
Kind of Business:	Selling religious and self-help books, CD's, and DVD's
Office Location:	From Home
Before Launching Business:	Family Crisis Counselor
Months to Profitability:	12
Unique Selling Proposition:	Most products are not available elsewhere
Challenges:	Constantly having to search for/find new inventory to sell
Internet Benefits:	Doesn't have to go to work any longer, Freedom
Hours Worked:	Full time
Advice to Others:	Sell items of familiarity and always keep learning
Monthly Income:	$1,000 per month (biggest month $2,800)

Name & Web site:	Lisa from Florida (www.TShirtsToo.com)
Kind of Business:	Selling t-shirts & stickers on Web (www.StickersEtc.com)
Office Location:	From home
Before Launching Business:	Housewife (husband was laid off so she started business)
Months to Profitability:	Three
Unique Selling Proposition:	No minimum volume requirement on shirts or stickers
Challenges:	Increased competition on the Web
Internet Benefits:	Can market services to the entire world
Hours Worked:	Full time
Advice to Others:	Focus on getting a high search engine placements
Monthly Income:	$1,000 per month (biggest month $20,000)

Name & Web site:	Cecilia from Florida (www.cjbisset.com)
Kind of Business:	Selling own artwork paintings (water color and pastels)
Office Location:	From home art studio
Before Launching Business:	Miscellaneous odd jobs
Months to Profitability:	One
Unique Selling Proposition:	Custom paintings that match client decor wishes
Challenges:	Keeping up with inventory; creating more paintings
Internet Benefits:	Conveniently can access global marketplace
Hours Worked:	Full time
Advice to Others:	Create Web site to market paintings and attend art shows
Monthly Income:	$3,000 per month (biggest month $22,000)

Name & Web site:	Vickie from California (www.VickieToy.com)
Kind of Business:	Selling stuffed animals and teddy bears on the Web
Office Location:	From Office Building
Before Launching Business:	Travel Agent
Months to Profitability:	Six
Unique Selling Proposition:	Never out of stock; ships product same day order is taken
Challenges:	Competing on price, quality, and style with competition
Internet Benefits:	Ability to market direct to the end customers worldwide
Hours Worked:	Full time (now ten employees)
Advice to Others:	Focus on search engine placement even though it costs $
Monthly Income:	$170,000 per month (Over $2 million per year)

As you can see, these are just regular folks taking advantage of the many benefits the Internet has to offer to produce additional income for their families. These folks are both part-time and full-time and are all marketing something they enjoy from the comfort of their home. However, all of them started part-time. These entrepreneurs are both men and women 25 to 75 years old.

I included an example of Vickie Toy Factory to show you the virtually unlimited income potential that Internet marketing has to offer. Vickie was an unhappy travel agent in 1995 before launching her company; now she has a team of ten employees and her company is doing over $2 million per year in revenues. Therefore, whether your goals are an extra $200 per month, or $2,000,000 per year, marketing your products and services via the Internet is an ideal vehicle to help you create your own destiny.

If a disgruntled travel agent with no advanced education or Internet training can earn two million dollars per year on the Internet selling teddy bears, then I believe virtually anyone regardless of their age or computer proficiency can make an extra $500 per month selling something they are passionate about on the Internet!

Getting started in business for yourself can be intimidating if you don't know exactly what you are doing. Therefore, I encourage you to seek out the assistance of a friend who has successfully launched a business. If you have a difficult time finding such a person, I have identified a couple of companies, such as Stores Online and EBAY, that can help you get started marketing your hobbies on the Internet.

SUMMARY

You are now at a point where you have learned the most important things for being successful in business. NOW it is time to take action and execute your plan *daily*! Conrad Hilton says that:

"Success seems to be connected with action.
Successful people keep moving.
They make mistakes, but they don't quit."

Just because you read a book about weight loss doesn't mean you are going to lose weight. You will only loose weight once you *implement the strategies* covered in the book. The same concept is true in business. Reading this book is not going to ensure that your business will be successful; you must take action, execute your plan, and implement the strategies covered in this chapter!

As you build your business and proceed forward, you are bound to come across obstacles that will overwhelm you at times and even force you to think about giving up. This is only natural; we all at times doubt our abilities. During these times, remember that the key to being successful in life and in business is to simply rise ONE more time than you fall. If you can commit to doing this, then you are destined to become a successful business owner!

If you have gotten this far in my book, I have no doubt you will be successful *when* you implement these strategies. I wish you all the success and freedom in the world that a successful business can provide you. America is a great country for many reasons, but I believe our FREE ENTERPRISE system is the best in the world and it's the primary reason why I encourage you to get started in your own business today!

I challenge you to implement all the strategies outlined in this chapter. Whether you start an Internet Marketing Business or any kind of business, it is important to note that the ideas, techniques, and strategies offered in this chapter are applicable to any kind of business that you launch. Regardless of the kind of business you decide to start, make sure it is in line with your passions!

CHAPTER 11

Developing Your Higher Calling

"When you were born, you cried and the world rejoiced! Live your life in a manner in which, when you die, the world cries and you rejoice!"
— Indian Saying

By now you should be well on the way to living your destiny: you know what it is that you want out of life, you're taking action on a daily basis, and you're prepared to overcome the obstacles, risks, and adversities that lie in your way. You will become a success; I'm certain of it. In fact, it was Henry David Thoreau who said:

"If one advances confidently in the direction of his dreams, and endeavors to live the life in which he has imagined, he will meet with a success unexpected in common hours."

Success will happen. When it comes, what are you going to do? Are you going to spend all your success on yourself?

Or are you going to give—of your time, your energy, and your money? When you do become a success—and in your life today—I'd like to press upon you a final thought: develop your higher calling.

WHAT IS A HIGHER CALLING?

It's something that you do above and beyond your destiny; it's the something, in other words, that you do to give back to the world.

For many, this might be faith; for others, it might be family or some other worthwhile cause. This higher calling is different for everyone, therefore I challenge you to seek out and develop yours.

Mother Teresa once said:

> **"I do not pray for success,
> I ask for faithfulness."**

She, arguably more than anyone, spent almost her entire life living out her higher calling by founding a convent in Calcutta, India, and devoting her life to helping the poor worldwide. When she died on September 5, 1997, I am sure she rejoiced at a time when the world cried!

Many professional athletes today come from a modest background. Once they make it to the big leagues they have the resources to give a tremendous amount of money back to their communities.

Take Alex Rodriquez, for example. He's a professional baseball player who played for the Seattle Mariners for seven years. I watched him come up through the ranks to become the game's premier shortstop in Major League Baseball. In the early 1990s, he was a high school student. After the 2000 season, he signed a new contract with the Texas Rangers for $252 million (before becoming a New York Yankee). That's right—more than a quarter of a billion dollars. That's a lot of money by anyone's count! With a higher calling combined with his looks, personality, charisma, and money, Alex Rodriquez can literally help impact the world for the better!

Alex has chosen to given literally millions of dollars of his money and countless hours of his time to the kids of inner-city Miami in an effort to help them overcome many of the adversities they face every day.

I know what you're probably thinking: It's easy to give money away and "make a difference" if you're a multi-millionaire.

That may be easy, but I also believe anyone can make a difference in the world regardless of how much you have to give. How? By giving of your time and energy as well.

Whether you realize it or not we are all capable of changing the world if each of us were to just reach out within our own communities and help feed, clothe, and nourish those in need. One person at a time, each of us can make a difference.

Read this poem by Randy Poole to see how you can make a difference regardless of your age, or your level of income. This poem will give you a whole new perspective on life. It will make you realize just how much of an impact one individual can have if they reach out and help others in need.

THE DIFFERENCE HE MADE

"Amidst the morning mist of the swift returning tide
I set out on my daily run, my Walkman on my side.
Lost within my private world apart from cares and woes
I ran along the moistened shore, the sand between my toes.

In the distance, I saw a boy, as busy as can be.
He was running, stooping, picking up, and tossing in the sea.
Just what he threw, I couldn't tell, I looked as I drew near.
It seemed to be a rock or shell—as I approached him I could hear.

'Back you go, where you belong. Your safe now hurry home.
Your family's waiting for you little starfish, hurry on!'
It seemed the evening tide had washed the starfish on the shore,
And the swift receding water left a thousand there or more.

And this self-appointed savior, was trying one-by-one
To toss them back into the sea, against the racing sun.
I saw his plight was hopeless, that most of them would die.
I called out from my private world, 'Hey Kid, why even try?'

'Must be a least a thousand here, strewn along the beach,
And even if you had the time, most you'll never reach.
You really think it makes a difference, to waste your time this way?'
And then I paused and waited, just to hear what he would say.

He stooped and took another, and looked me in the eye.
'It makes a difference to this one sir, this starfish will not die!'
With that, he tossed the little life, back where there was hope.
He stooped to take another. I could tell this was no joke.

The words that he spoke to me cut like a surgeon's knife.
Where I saw only numbers, he saw only life.
He didn't see the multitude of starfish on the sand.
He only saw the little life he held there in his hand.

He didn't stop to argue, to prove that he was right.
He just kept tossing starfish in the sea with all his might.
So I too stooped, and picked up, and I tossed into the sea,
And I thought, just what a difference, that this boy has made in me."

Now consider ways you can learn from the boy in the starfish poem and help improve your family, your community, and the world:

- Spending more time at home with your family
- Volunteering for neighborhood or community boards or committees
- Becoming involved in a world-wide "cause"
- Coaching a kids' sports team
- Donating food to food banks
- Donating money or clothes to worthy organizations
- Volunteering your time in a church group
- Even just saving sea life that has been washed ashore

EXERCISE

Reflect for a moment, then list all the potential ways you can "make a difference" in the world.

_____

_____

_____

_____

_____

_____

_____

_____

The opportunities to make a difference are numerous. What's more, they're all around you. Seek them out, then devote your time, energy, passion, and—if you can—your money. I am currently developing my higher calling. You may not know what your higher calling is yet—but thinking about a higher calling is a good start. I have two boys, and through them I have learned how much I enjoy children. Therefore, it disturbs me to learn that, according to UNICEF, each year 6 million children around the world die because of malnutrition.

My higher calling is guided by my faith and is dedicated to helping the children of the world who are in need. I am helping influence the youth of today to become the leaders of tomorrow!

S. Truett Cathy, founder of Chick-fil-A and foster parent to more than 120 children, has inspired my higher calling, which is to own and operate foster homes for children in need. I want to help these children avoid addictions of drugs and alcohol and help them become the leaders of tomorrow.

Additionally, I have partnered with a world-class organization called Performance Dynamics (www.PerformanceDynamics.net). Founded by two visionaries, Ashoke and Kris Menon, Performance Dynamics shares my vision for helping the youth of today become the leaders of tomorrow. It is making a huge difference in our world by marketing leadership and mentoring programs to schools throughout North America. To learn more information about Performance Dynamics and to support or join our vision, please visit the Web site or call (866) 260-5036.

Ashoke and Kris Menon's new book will soon be released so that you can read about the lasting impact that their work is having on the youth of North America. One child at a time they are making a huge difference!

EXERCISE

What is your higher calling in life?

_____

_____

_____

_____

_____

DEFINITION OF SUCCESS

We've talked a great deal in this chapter about success, and your higher calling. Those are great, worthy topics. But I'd like you to consider this thought: achieving your destiny and obtaining success are never endpoints, never something you can obtain and then never find again. Ben Sweetland has said that:

"Success is a journey, not a destination."

To make your journey in life a fulfilling one, consider this <u>definition of success</u> by an unknown source:

- **To laugh often and much**
- **To win the respect of intelligent people, and the affection of young children**

- To appreciate beauty

- To seek out the best in others

- To leave the world a better place, whether by a healthy child, a garden patch, or a redeemed social condition

- To know that even one life has breathed easier because you have lived

Castaway starring Tom Hanks, is one of my favorite movies as it symbolizes the essence of "choice," better than any other movie that I have ever seen. While everyone was so caught up in the plane crash and his living on a deserted island for so long, I was impacted the most at the end of the movie after he delivered the last package. At this point, while very far out in the middle of no where, he came to a crossroads. He looked in each direction as far as the eye could see. And in doing so, for maybe the first time in his life, he was able to CHOOSE which road to travel. For probably the first time in his life, he used his heart as his compass, to choose which direction to travel. I challenge you to do the same. I believe that if you listen to your heart and then choose your own destiny, you will then also pursue a higher calling at the same time. In which direction do you choose to go? This is your choice regardless of the other influences in your life!

This scene at the end of the movie reminds me of what J. Martin Kohe once said:

"The greatest power that a person possesses is the power to choose."

SUMMARY

Now that you have almost completed this book, you, too, may be at a crossroads. I challenge you to travel down the road that your heart desires. But remember, whichever road you choose, please go in a manner in which our world will be a better place because of you, and what you have given back!

Here's another quote by T. Menlo which I believe best illustrates the concept of developing a higher calling:

"If each day of your life represents a sparkle of light, at your life's end you will have illuminated the world."

To each of you reading this book, you individually (not anyone else) will sooner or later need to determine what your higher calling is in life. It will be different for each of us, but I hope that you identify it—and that you devote your life to helping others in a way which no one else can!

As you develop your higher calling and give back to the world and to those in need, you will ultimately become a more fulfilled individual and also experience more *love* and more *happiness* as a result of your efforts.

I challenge you to seek out your higher calling, and then illuminate the world on your journey along the way. You are doing great things; you are about to do even greater things. Enjoy life, and live every day by treating it like the precious gift that it really is! I would like to end this chapter with a quote from Charles Dickens:

"No one is useless in this world who lightens the burden of it for anyone else."

CHAPTER 12

Asking Yourself The Ultimate Destiny Questions

"Aim at heaven and you will get earth thrown in. Aim at earth and you will get neither."

— C.S. Lewis

What is your ultimate destiny? What happens to you after your time on earth is through? This book is not a book on theology! In fact I struggled with whether or not I should even include this section in my book. All of the so-called experts advised me not to bring up the issue of God for fear that it could turn away some readers. I am not a minister, nor am I even qualified to write about faith and the belief in God (or lack there of). As a result, you will see no other mention of this topic anywhere else in this book.

However, in thinking over this issue, I finally decided that I would be doing my readers a major disservice to write a book about destiny, and not pose the above questions! Therefore, I have decided to include this section in my book and will share with you my beliefs on faith, since so many of my readers have inquired as to what I believe.

With this being the case, I want to challenge you. My challenge is for you to search for your beliefs about your creator and your ultimate destiny. Without God, I believe that much of life does not make sense, and your search for a greater meaning will continue endlessly. For example, many people search for fulfillment in the wrong places with the zealous pursuit of money and through material consumption.

But with God, I believe that true fulfillment in life is attainable! I also believe that God ultimately decides our final destiny in life. However, it doesn't really matter what I believe. What is important here is for you to determine what your beliefs are, what has shaped and influenced your beliefs over time, and why you feel the way you do. Do you believe in God? Do you believe in life after death? On the back of this book, you will see my quote stating:

**"Only those who can see the invisible,
can accomplish the impossible.
The BELIEF in your VISION is the key
to Creating Your Own Destiny."**

To many people, God is invisible. But for those who can see God's presence, their faith and belief will bring them fulfillment and allow them to do great things in life while making a huge contribution to this world! If you have a belief in God and in your own vision, you will become unstoppable in life and repeatedly create a greater good for humanity. I believe that with God, all things are possible!

However, some people argue that it is not honorable to strive for great achievements on earth if you want to shape your ultimate destiny in God's eye. My view on this issue is that it is important to strive for both. Live your life in a way in which you work hard to attain your goals, but while doing so, continuously look for ways to give back and help others in need. The previous chapter of this book was designed to address this concern.

Let me share with you how I have become the person am I today, in case you are wondering how I arrived at this point in my life with regards to my faith. When I was 17 years old, as you recall my goal was to play in the NFL. Therefore, the summer before graduating from High School, I attended a Fellowship of Christian Athletes sports camp, where I selected football as my sport of emphasis.

During this week, in addition to football, I was exposed to Jesus Christ (in a way that I had never been before). As a result, I soon realized that even if I were to achieve my goal of making it to the pros, and perhaps even winning a Super Bowl ring, that the exhilaration of winning a championship on earth would only be temporary.

However, by following Christ, I realized that a championship with God in heaven would last an eternity! As a result of this revelation, I accepted Jesus Christ in my heart as my personal Lord and Savior during the summer of 1986. Since then, he has been my co-pilot and has steered me toward my true destiny in life of helping others succeed. I believe that my life is a gift from God, and that my gift back to God is what I make of my life.

I hope that in writing _Creating Your Own Destiny_ I have helped you on your journey in life, and that you ponder this message on faith as my gift to you! I am NOT trying to tell you what to believe, I am just telling you what I believe, and how following Christ has positively impacted my life!

With the presence of God in your heart, I believe you can help shape your ultimate destiny in life. I challenge you to seek out your faith so that you can have God at your side, as you travel along your journey in pursuit of your goals—both in your life on earth, and beyond!

EXERCISE

What are your beliefs about God?

_____

_____

_____

_____

What are your beliefs about life after death?

_____

_____

_____

_____

What events in your life have shaped your beliefs on this subject?

_____

_____

_____

_____

What is your ultimate destiny?

_____

_____

_____

_____

Achieving Your Destiny

"Thoughts lead on to purposes, purposes go forth in action, action forms habits, habits decide character, and character fixes our destiny."

— Tryon Edwards

W ell, this has been my story. I hope that in some way you have been inspired and have benefited from my thoughts and suggestions! After reading this book, I am hopeful that you will now believe what William Jennings Bryant once said:

**"Destiny is not a matter of chance,
it is a matter of choice.
It is not a thing to be waited for,
it is a thing to be achieved."**

As I close, I want you to understand that life is full of choices, and that you must take charge of your life by choosing your destiny and moving forward with confidence and determination! Always remember what Yogi Berra said:

**"If you don't know where you are going,
you are bound to end up somewhere else!"**

I am hopeful that my material in this book has inspired you to further discover the destiny for which you were born! If not, I challenge you to consistently go through my **Success**

Road Map to help guide your way in this challenging world that we all live:

SUCCESS ROAD MAP

1. **Visualize Your Dreams**
2. **Set Big Goals**
3. **Create Your Game Plan**
4. **Build Real Wealth**
5. **Put Your Family Ahead of Work**
6. **Conquer Adversity, Temptation, & Addiction**
7. **Overcome Your Fears**
8. **Remember Those Who Molded You**
9. **Execute Your Plan Daily**
10. **Launch Your New Business**
11. **Develop Your Higher Calling**
12. **Ask Yourself The Ultimate Destiny Questions**

The point of this whole soul-searching process—and my book specifically—is to simply help you understand that the destiny we are all born with, is that we all share the same freedom to choose whether or not to take control of our lives. The only way to take control of our lives is through our GOALS!

We can take control of our lives and destiny...*simply by writing out our future in advance!* By doing so, we can **create our own destiny!** After all, it was Peter Drucker who said:

"The best way to predict the future is to create it."

I urge you to get started immediately by taking advantage of the freedom that we all enjoy, and decide once and for all:

**EXACTLY WHAT IT IS IN LIFE
THAT YOU WANT!**

Once you have finally discovered your destiny, I challenge you to plow forward and DEVELOP THE COURAGE to pursue it by taking action and executing your game plan on a daily basis.

I have developed this book to act as your road map and compass, to help direct and guide you as you pursue your life goals. I *challenge* you to incorporate my ideas, techniques, and strategies summarized in this book, so that you will ultimately experience what most people want—more *time*, more *money*, more *freedom*, more *health*, more *love*, and more *happiness*!

Some people spend their whole life preparing to live, but they never live. Even though much of this book is about planning your future in advance, I still think it is extremely important to enjoy the present moment and live today. It was Henry Van Dyke who said in his poem *Seize the Day*:

**"Be glad of life, because it gives you
the chance to love and to work, and
to play and to look up at the stars"**

If you execute your plan daily and pursue your goals and destiny, make absolutely certain that you want what it is that you are pursuing! Dale Carnegie said it best:

**"Success is getting what you want,
happiness is wanting what you get."**

Now that you have completed this book, I am hopeful that you are ready to fully comprehend my **Success Secret** that I eluded to in the Introduction. This secret has become my personal philosophy. It is something that I have developed after almost 20 years of intense study in the field of personal growth and development.

This secret, if adopted in your life, will be all the knowledge that you need to discover what my subtitle of this book promises:

*"How to Get Exactly What **You** Want Out of Life."*

At 2:30 a.m. on the morning of March 16, 2002, I had a revelation and I woke up out of a deep sleep to write this **Success Secret** (see page 229).

If you take nothing more away from my book always remember two things: my **Success Secret**, and what author, Nobel and Pulitzer Prize Winner Pearl S. Buck has said:

"The young do not know enough to be prudent, and therefore they attempt the impossible— and achieve it generation after generation."

Whether you are young or old, if your belief in your vision is strong enough, you can accomplish the impossible time and time again! You are a living magnet and you attract that which you envision. Whatever you want, wants you!

No where in this book did I mention that creating your own destiny would be easy, or without your share of pain. In fact, achieving one's destiny may be one of the most difficult challenges that we ultimately face in life. However, I am a firm believer in what Tour de France champion and cancer survivor, Lance Armstrong, says about pursuing one's dreams in his book, *Every Second Counts*:

"Be brave and fight like hell! Pain is temporary but quitting lasts forever."

I challenge you to never give up in pursuing your destiny and fight as if your life depended on it—because it does! Ultimately, I would argue that your level of happiness in life is partly dependent on whether or not you stay true to your dreams. Always remember that it is not over, until you win! Winning takes commitment and determination. Poet, Henry Wadsworth Longfellow said:

"The heights by great men achieved and kept,
were not attained by a sudden fight,
but while their companions slept,
kept toiling upward in the night."

Creating your own destiny is a life-long battle within your mind to take action on your dreams. It is a battle, nonetheless, that you will win with intention and persistence!

Now that you know my story and have learned my destiny, I am hopeful that you will contact me to share what your dreams are in life. Perhaps, I can help coach you to achieve your destiny.

I further challenge you to…

DREAM, PLAN, EXECUTE, & SOAR!

May your life be filled with peace, love, prosperity, and the achievement of your destiny!

Thank you and God bless.

I appreciate you!

Your friend:

SUCCESS SECRET

"Once you decide what it is that you really want out of life, <u>your mind</u> will be your ONLY obstacle.

When you start to believe and trust in yourself and in your own unique passions, you will conquer your mind's current self-limiting beliefs. These limiting beliefs are the only roadblock or obstacle that can hold you back from getting all of what it is that you really want.

Once you have made this decision to overcome your fears, conquer all of your self-doubt, and have won this battle of the mind, you will accomplish everything that you have ever envisioned.

Your mind will have ignited a fire in your heart to execute your plan by taking daily actions in pursuit of your goals. As you experience this, you will become an unstoppable force of power, fully capable of achieving more success and freedom than you could have ever imagined.

Once you have done this, you will literally, Create Your Own Destiny!"

— Patrick Snow

www.CreateYourOwnDestiny.com
(800) 951-7721

ABOUT THE AUTHOR

For more than 20 years, Patrick Snow has studied the field of personal growth and development. As a result, he has been called "The Dean of Destiny" by high achievers nationwide and today is an author, speaker, coach, and entrepreneur. Patrick has become a leading authority on how to discover and create your ultimate destiny in life! His destiny message was featured on the cover story of *USA Today*. His message has also been featured in the *Chicago Sun-Times*, and *The Denver Post*, as well as on more than 300 radio stations throughout North America and Europe.

Patrick is author of *Creating Your Own Destiny: How to Get Exactly What You Want Out of Life* which has sold more than 60,000 copies since its first printing in July of 2001. He is a co-author of *Inspiring Breakthrough Secrets to Live Your Dreams* and a contributing author to *Wake Up...Live the Life You Love* along with Robert Allen, Mark Victor Hansen, Cynthia Kersey, and Dr. Wayne Dyer.

Patrick has been tracking layoffs and worker discontent for years. As a Business-Ownership Advocate, Patrick's mission in life is to help others turn their career distress, into personal success through business ownership.

Originally from Michigan, Patrick graduated from the University of Montana in 1991, and has lived in the Seattle area for more than 12 years. He and his wife, Cheryl, currently reside on Bainbridge Island, Washington, along with their two boys, Samuel and Jacob. He volunteers his time in the community by coaching youth sports and counseling troubled youth.

About The Snow Group, Inc.

After 10 years of speaking to various organizations on a part-time basis, Patrick Snow has successfully launched The Snow Group in January of 2000. He is committed to helping those who are unhappy at work and want to get more out of life by turning their career distress, into personal success!

Patrick is accepting new clientele in the following areas:

Publishing .... Marketing ideas to help others succeed in life

Motivational Speaking .... Customizing keynote speeches for meeting planners

Success Coaching .... Assisting unhappy workers to get started in business

Publishing Coaching .... Getting manuscripts easily published without the hassles

Speaker Coaching .... Advising speakers on how to get paid as a professional

Author Coaching .... Teaching authors how to sell more books and make money

Entrepreneurial Training ..... Providing business opportunities

For a no-obligation, 30-minute **FREE** consultation, please call or e-mail:

The Snow Group, Inc
P.O. Box 10864
Bainbridge Island, WA 98110
(800) 951-7721
www.CreateYourOwnDestiny.com
Patrick@CreateYourOwnDestiny.com

RECOMMENDED READING

A Life on the Edge – Jim Whittaker
Break Through to a LIFE that ROX – Larry Olsen
Chicken Soup For The Soul (entire series) – Jack Canfield and Mark Victor Hansen
Creating Your Own Destiny – Patrick Snow
Do What You Love and the Money Will Follow – Marsha Sinetar
Don't Sweat the Small Stuff – Richard Carlson
Drive Yourself Happy – Dr. Rhonda Hull
Eat Mor Chikin Inspire More People – S. Truett Cathy
Every Second Counts – Lance Armstrong
Failing Forward – John C. Maxwell
Grow Rich with Peace of Mind – Napoleon Hill
Hope for Each Day – Billy Graham
How to Win Friends and Influence People – Dale Carnegie
If You THINK You CAN! – T.J. Hoisington
Inspiring Breakthrough Secrets to Live Your Dreams – co-authored by Patrick Snow
Jump Start Your Business Brain – Doug Hall
Life Is Tremendous – Charlie Jones
Live Your Dreams – Les Brown
Love is the Killer App – Tim Sanders
Man's Search for Himself – Rollo May
Million Dollar Habits – Robert Ringer
Multiple Streams of Income – Robert Allen
Rich Dad Poor Dad – Robert Kiyosaki
Rudy's Rules – Rudy Ruettiger
See You at the Top – Zig Ziglar
Simple Steps to Impossible Dreams – Steven Scott
Swim With the Sharks without Being Eaten Alive – Harvey Mackay
The Automatic Millionaire – David Bach
The Bible – Multiple Authors
The Cashflow Quadrant – Robert Kiyosaki
The Code: The 5 Secrets to Teen Success – Mawi Asgedom
The Millionaire Next Door – Thomas Stanley and William Danko
The One Minute Millionaire – Mark Victor Hansen and Robert Allen
The Purpose Driven Life – Rick Warren
The Spellbinders Gift – Og Mandino
The Success Principles – Jack Canfield
The 7 Habits of Highly Effective People – by Stephen Covey
The 21 Irrefutable Laws of Leadership – John C. Maxwell
Think & Grow Rich – Napoleon Hill
Unlimited Power – Anthony Robbins
Unstoppable – Cynthia Kersey
Wake Up...Live the Life You Love – Steven E and 107 Contributing Authors
Way of the Peaceful Warrior – Dan Millman
When the Drumbeat Changes, Dance a Different Dance – Albert Mensah
Who Moved My Cheese – Spencer Johnson
Working Wounded – Bob Rosner

**To order additional copies of this book
within North America call:
(800) 431-1579**

Outside of North America call:
(914) 835-0015

To book Patrick Snow
to speak to your organization call:
(800) 951-7721

To see a video clip of Patrick Snow,
please visit his Web site below
and click on "Media Gallery."

To receive Patrick Snow's *Destiny* Newsletter
please visit his Web site and enter your
e-mail address. This Newsletter comes
once a month and is full of inspiring
quotes as well as success strategies.

www.CreateYourOwnDestiny.com

"Only those who can see the invisible,
can accomplish the impossible!
The BELIEF in your VISION is the key to
Creating Your Own Destiny."
— Patrick Snow

Quick Order Form

Fax: (206) 780-8175 *(send this form or a copy of this form)*

Call: (800) 431-1579 *(international call (914) 835-0015)*

Web: www.CreateYourOwnDestiny.com

Write: The Snow Group – P.O. Box 10864
Bainbridge Island, WA 98110

❏ Please send me _____ copies of *Creating Your Own Destiny*
at $14.95 each, plus shipping and handling.

❏ Please send me _____ copies of *Inspiring Breakthrough Secrets*
at $19.95 each, plus shipping and handling.

❏ Please send me _____ copies of *Wake Up...Live the Life You Love*
at $14.95 each, plus shipping and handling.

❏ Please send me _____ copies of *Destiny Journal Workbook*
at $29.95 each, plus shipping and handling.

❏ Please send me _____ copies of *Creating Your Own Destiny*
(audiobook) at $14.95 each, plus shipping and handling.

❏ Please send me _____ copies of *Creating Your Own Destiny*
(video) at $29.95 each, plus shipping and handling.

Name: _____ Date: _____

Address: _____

City: _____ State: _____ Zip: _____

Phone: _____

Email address: _____

Sales tax: Please add 8.2% for products shipped to Washington addresses.
Shipping: US: $4 for the first book and $2 for each additional book.
International: Based on ship-to location and current rates; call for exact amounts.

Payment type: ❏ Check   ❏ Visa   ❏ Mastercard

Credit card #: _____

Name on card: _____ exp date: _____ / _____

Signature: _____

**To book Patrick for motivational speaking, success coaching,
or sales training, please call (800) 951-7721 or visit his Web site at:
www.CreateYourOwnDestiny.com**

**To order additional copies of this book
within North America call:
(800) 431-1579**

Outside of North America call:
(914) 835-0015

To book Patrick Snow
to speak to your organization call:
(800) 951-7721

To see a video clip of Patrick Snow,
please visit his Web site below
and click on "Media Gallery."

To receive Patrick Snow's _Destiny_ Newsletter
please visit his Web site and enter your
e-mail address. This Newsletter comes
once a month and is full of inspiring
quotes as well as success strategies.

www.CreateYourOwnDestiny.com

"Only those who can see the invisible,
can accomplish the impossible!
The BELIEF in your VISION is the key to
Creating Your Own Destiny."
— Patrick Snow

Quick Order Form

Fax: (206) 780-8175 *(send this form or a copy of this form)*

Call: (800) 431-1579 *(international call (914) 835-0015)*

Web: www.CreateYourOwnDestiny.com

Write: The Snow Group – P.O. Box 10864
Bainbridge Island, WA 98110

❑ Please send me _____ copies of *Creating Your Own Destiny* at $14.95 each, plus shipping and handling.

❑ Please send me _____ copies of *Inspiring Breakthrough Secrets* at $19.95 each, plus shipping and handling.

❑ Please send me _____ copies of *Wake Up…Live the Life You Love* at $14.95 each, plus shipping and handling.

❑ Please send me _____ copies of *Destiny Journal Workbook* at $29.95 each, plus shipping and handling.

❑ Please send me _____ copies of *Creating Your Own Destiny* (audiobook) at $14.95 each, plus shipping and handling.

❑ Please send me _____ copies of *Creating Your Own Destiny* (video) at $29.95 each, plus shipping and handling.

Name: _____ Date: _____

Address: _____

City: _____ State: _____ Zip: _____

Phone: _____

Email address: _____

Sales tax: Please add 8.2% for products shipped to Washington addresses.
Shipping: US: $4 for the first book and $2 for each additional book.
International: Based on ship-to location and current rates; call for exact amounts.

Payment type: ❑ Check ❑ Visa ❑ Mastercard

Credit card #: _____

Name on card: _____ exp date: ____ / ____

Signature: _____

To book Patrick for motivational speaking, success coaching, or sales training, please call (800) 951-7721 or visit his Web site at: www.CreateYourOwnDestiny.com